Abraham Lincoln

Carl Shurz

Contents

BIOGRAPHICAL SKETCH OF CARL SCHULZ. 7
CHRONOLOGICAL LIST OF EVENTS IN THE LIFE OF ABRAHAM LINCOLN......... 10
REMARKS AT THE FUNERAL SERVICES HELD IN CONCORD, APRIL 19, 1865. 54
THE EMANCIPATION GROUP. BY JOHN GEEENLEAF WHITTIER. 58
FOR THE SEEVICES IN MEMOEY OF ABEAHAM LINCOLN. 59

ABRAHAM LINCOLN

BY

Carl Shurz

BIOGRAPHICAL SKETCH OF CARL SCHULZ.

It is interesting to note that one of the best studies of an American statesman and the best brief summary of Abraham Lincoln's career came from the hand of one born out of the country; for the fact points two ways,—it indicates the hospitality of America, and it intimates how great a contribution the rest of the world is constantly making to the development of American life. We sometimes think and speak as if Americans and American institutions all sprang from the colonization which took place from England in the seventeenth century, forgetting that the nineteenth century has seen a far more extensive and more varied migration from all Europe.

Carl Schurz was born March 2, 1829, near Cologne, Prussia, and was a student in the University of Bonn in 1848, when the revolutionary movement in Germany drew to itself many enthusiastic young men who thought they saw the opportunity for the establishment of republican principles. The movement was quickly suppressed by the existing government, and led to the exile of some of the most promising men of intellectual powers. Many came to this country and found positions in colleges and universities. One of the conspicuous men was Francis Lieber, who continued his academic life and was long a force as a political thinker and writer. Another was Carl Schurz, who, with more of the qualities of a public man, began at once, on coming to this country in 1852, to prepare himself for active life. He knew little or no English when he landed, but in three years he had so mastered the study of law that he was admitted to the bar in Jefferson, Wisconsin. He found himself amongst his former countrymen in the Northwest, and at once threw himself ardently into politics in sympathy with the movement against the extension of slavery.

So rapidly did he come to the front that he was candidate for the office of Lieutenant-Governor of Wisconsin in 1857, and came within two hundred votes of an election. In the great debate between Lincoln and Douglas in 1858, he joined himself to Lincoln and took an active part in that political campaign. That was the beginning of his friendship with Lincoln; and though as chairman of the Wisconsin delegation to the convention in 1860, he persistently advocated the nomination of Mr. Seward, he accepted heartily the choice of Lincoln, and from that time till the election was incessantly working for him and addressing political meetings.

Mr. Lincoln set so high a value on Mr. Schurz's worth that he appointed him Minister to Spain. At the time, he was actively engaged in organizing the first cavalry regiment of volunteers; and when after a few months at Madrid he returned to lay before the administration the result of his observation of the political attitude of European governments, he was appointed Brigadier-General, and a few months later Major-General, and served in the field till the end of the war.

His clear intelligence of public affairs was recognized in his appointment by President Johnson as special commissioner to report on the condition of the seaboard and Gulf States. His report had great weight with Congress in its subsequent legislation, but Mr. Schurz made his political judgment still more effective in the years of reconstruction by his writings as a journalist. Successively a special correspondent of *The New York Tribune* and editor of the *Detroit Post,* he became in 1867 part owner and editor of the Westliche Post of St. Louis. So strong a power did he now become that in 1869 he was elected United States senator from Missouri.

He was, however, a man who held firmly to what he conceived to be political principles when they came into conflict with party policy, and he threw himself into the movement known as the Liberal Republican party in 1872. In 1876 he returned to the support of the Republican party, and President Hayes invited him into his cabinet as Secretary of the Interior. His administration of that office afforded a fresh illustration of his application of political principles to conduct. He had identified himself with the movement for the reform of the civil service, and being now in a position where he could put his belief into practice, he made the department a witness to the efficacy of the merit system, and gave a striking object lesson of the possibility of carrying on the government on this basis.

At the close of Mr. Hayes's administration Mr. Schurz abandoned official life, and returned to journalism, giving also a few years to business, but he did not abandon the public service. An independent in politics, he continued to give his powerful influence, in speech and in writing, on all the great political questions, maintaining a devotion to high ideals, so that it is doubtful if any private citizen in the last twenty years has been listened to more attentively. When the seventieth anniversary of his birthday came, there was a large popular expression of gratitude and admiration.

One source of Mr. Schurz's influence may be traced to the singular ability with which he has made himself at home in American political history. Another German, Dr. Von Holst, has also shown this remarkable faculty, but Dr. Von Holst has been especially a political philosopher; Mr. Schurz has been a political historian, and his "Henry Clay," in the American Statesmen series, displays an intimate familiarity with the ins and outs of politics. He has written it from an American, not a German-American point of view; and it is this identification of himself with his adopted country, illustrated also by his idiomatic use of the English language, while yet retaining the power of speaking freely in his mother tongue to his former countrymen, which lies at the basis of his moral influence. He brought an ardent love of free institutions with him when he came to this country, and he has always lived enveloped with this atmosphere while having a firm hold of the soil of American life.

Slight as the sketch is which follows, it has a double value. It is a fine, discriminating analysis of Lincoln's greatness, couched in a strong, lucid style, and it reflects a habit of mind which political students may wisely cultivate: the habit, that is, of referring political careers to standards of righteousness and not of expediency. Such a habit is of untold worth in a democratic country like America, where the disposition, inherent in the political consciousness, of accepting the judgment of the majority is liable to be misled into a too hasty following of the crowd which is making the loudest noise.

CHRONOLOGICAL LIST OF EVENTS IN THE LIFE OF ABRAHAM LINCOLN.

Born in a log-cabin near Hodgensville, now Larue County, Kentucky February 12, 1809
7 His father moves with his family into the wilderness near Gentryville, Indiana 1816
9 His mother dies, at the age of 35   1818
10 His fatherŽs second marriage 1819
17 Walks nine miles a day, going and returning to school   1826
19 Makes a trip to New Orleans and back, at work on a flat-boat   1828
20 Drives in an ox-cart with his father and stepmother to a clearing
    on the Sangamon River, near Decatur, Illinois   1829
20 Splits rails, to surround the clearing with a fence   1829
20 Makes another flat-boat trip to New Orleans and back, on
    which trip he first sees negroes shackled together in chains, and forms his
    opinions concerning slavery   May, 1831
22 Begins work in a store at New Salem, Illinois   August, 1831
23 Enlists in the Black Hawk War; elected a captain of volunteers   1832
23 Announces himself a Whig candidate for the Legislature, and is defeated   1832
24 Storekeeper, Postmaster, and Surveyor 1833
25 Elected to the Illinois Legislature   1834
26-33 Re lected to the Legislature 1835 to 1842
28 Studies law at Springfield   1837
31 Is a Presidential elector on the Whig national ticket   1840
33 Marries Mary Todd November 4, 1842
35 Canvasses Illinois for Henry Clay   1844
37 Elected to Congress 1846
39 Supports General Taylor for President 1848
40-45 Engages in law practice   1849-1854
46 Debates with Douglas at Peoria and Springfield 1855
46-47 Aids in organizing the Republican party   1855-1856
49 Joint debates in Illinois with Stephen A. Douglas   1858
50 Makes political speeches in Ohio   1859
51 Visits New York, and speaks at Cooper Union February,   1860
51 Attends Republican State Convention at Decatur; declared to be
    the choice of Illinois for the Presidency   May, 1860
51 Nominated at Chicago as the Republican candidate for President   May 16, 1860
51 Elected President over J. C. Breckenridge, Stephen A. Douglas, and John Bell November, 1860
52 Inaugurated President   March 4 1861

52 Issues first order for troops to put down the Rebellion, April 15, 1861
53 Urges McClellan to advance April, 1862
53 Appeals for the support of border States to the Union cause, March to July, 1862
53 Calls for 300,000 more troops July, 1862
53 Issues Emancipation Proclamation January 1, 1863
54 Thanks Grant for capture of Vicksburg July, 1863
54 His address at Gettysburg November 19, 1863
55 Calls for 500,000 volunteers July, 1864
55 Renominated and Reelected President 1864
55 Thanks Sherman for capture of Atlanta September, 1864
56 His second inauguration March 4, 1865
56 Assassinated April 14, 1865

By CARL SCHURZ.

No American can study the character and career of Abraham Lincoln without being carried away by sentimental emotions. We are always inclined to idealize that which we love,—a state of mind very unfavorable to the exercise of sober critical judgment. It is therefore not surprising that most of those who have written or spoken on that extraordinary man, even while conscientiously endeavoring to draw a life-like portraiture of his being, and to form a just estimate of his public conduct, should have drifted into more or less indiscriminating eulogy, painting his great features in the most glowing colors, and covering with tender shadings whatever might look like a blemish.

But his standing before posterity will not be exalted by mere praise of his virtues and abilities, nor by any concealment of his limitations and faults. The stature of the great man, one of whose peculiar charms consisted in his being so unlike all other great men, will rather lose than gain by the idealization which so easily runs into the commonplace. For it was distinctly the weird mixture of qualities and forces in him, of the lofty with the common, the ideal with the uncouth, of that which he had become with that which he had not ceased to be, that made him so fascinating a character among his fellow men, gave him his singular power over their minds and hearts, and fitted him to be the greatest leader in the greatest crisis of our national life.

His was indeed a marvellous growth. The statesman or the military hero born and reared in a log cabin is a familiar figure in American history; but we may search in vain among our celebrities for one whose origin and early life equalled Abraham Lincoln's in wretchedness. He first saw the light in a miserable hovel in Kentucky, on a farm consisting of a few barren acres in a dreary neighborhood; his father a typical "poor Southern white," shiftless and improvident, without ambition for himself or his children, constantly looking for a new piece of land on which he might make a living without much work; his mother, in her youth handsome and bright, grown prematurely coarse in feature and soured in mind by daily toil and care; the whole household squalid, cheerless, and utterly void of elevating inspirations. Only when the family had "moved" into the malarious backwoods of Indiana, the mother had died, and a stepmother, a woman of thrift and energy, had taken charge of the children, the shaggy-headed, ragged, barefooted, forlorn boy, then seven years old, "began to feel like a human being." Hard work was his early lot. When a mere boy he had to help in supporting the family, either on his father's clearing, or hired out to other farmers to plough, or dig ditches, or chop wood, or drive ox teams; occasionally also to "tend the baby" when the farmer's wife was otherwise engaged. He could regard it as an advancement to a higher sphere of activity when he obtained work in a "cross-roads store," where he amused the customers by his talk over the counter; for he soon distinguished himself among the backwoods folk as one who had something to say worth listening to. To win that distinction, he had to draw mainly upon his wits; for while his thirst for knowledge was great, his opportunities for satisfying that thirst were woefully slender.

In the log schoolhouse, which he could visit but little, he was taught only reading, writing, and elementary arithmetic. Among the people of the settlement, bush farmers and small tradesmen, he found none of uncommon intelligence or education; but some of them had a few books, which he borrowed eagerly. Thus he read and re-read Æsop's Fables, learning to tell stories with a point and to argue by parables; he read Robinson Crusoe, The Pilgrim's Progress, a short history of the United States, and Weems's Life of Washington. To the town constable's he went to read the Revised Statutes of Indiana. Every printed page that fell into his hands he would greedily devour, and his family and friends watched him with wonder, as the uncouth boy, after his daily work, crouched in a corner of the log cabin or outside under a tree, absorbed in a book while munching his supper of corn bread. In this manner he began to gather some knowledge, and sometimes he would astonish the girls with such startling remarks as that the earth was moving around the sun, and not the sun around the earth, and they marvelled where "Abe" could have got such queer notions. Soon he also felt the impulse to write, not only making extracts from books he wished to remember, but also composing little essays of his own. First he sketched these with charcoal on a wooden shovel scraped white with a drawing-knife, or on basswood shingles. Then he transferred them to paper, which was a scarce commodity in the Lincoln household, taking care to cut his expressions close, so that they might not cover too much space,—a style-forming method greatly to be commended. Seeing boys put a burning coal on the back of a wood turtle, he was moved to write on cruelty to animals. Seeing men intoxicated with whiskey, he wrote on temperance. In verse-making, too, he tried himself, and in satire on persons offensive to him or others,—satire the rustic wit of which was not always fit for ears polite. Also political thoughts he put upon paper, and some of his pieces were even deemed good enough for publication in the county weekly.

Thus he won a neighborhood reputation as a clever young man, which he increased by his performances as a speaker, not seldom drawing upon himself the dissatisfaction of his employers by mounting a stump in the field, and keeping the farm hands from their work by little speeches in a jocose and sometimes also a serious vein. At the rude social frolics of the settlement he became an important person, telling funny stories, mimicking the itinerant preachers who had happened to pass by, and making his mark at wrestling matches, too; for at the age of seventeen he had attained his full height, six feet four inches in his stockings, if he had any, and a terribly muscular clodhopper he was. But he was known never to use his extraordinary strength to the injury or humiliation of others; rather to do them a kindly turn, or to enforce justice and fair dealing between them. All this made him a favorite in backwoods society, although in some things he appeared a little odd to his friends. Far more than any of them, he was given, not only to reading, but to fits of abstraction, to quiet musing with himself, and also to strange spells of melancholy, from which he often would pass in a moment to rollicking outbursts of droll humor. But on the whole he was one of the people among whom he lived; in appearance perhaps even a little more uncouth than most of them,—a very tall, rawboned youth, with large features, dark, shrivelled skin, and rebellious hair; his arms and legs long, out of proportion; clad in deerskin trousers, which from frequent exposure to the rain had shrunk so as to sit tightly on his limbs, leaving several inches of bluish shin exposed between their lower end and the heavy tan-colored shoes; the nether garment held usually by only one suspender, that was strung over a coarse home-made shirt; the head covered in winter with a coonskin cap, in summer with a rough straw hat of uncertain shape, without a band.

It is doubtful whether he felt himself much superior to his surroundings, although he confessed to a yearning for some knowledge of the world outside of the circle in which he lived. This wish was gratified; but how? At the age of nineteen he went down the Mississippi to New Orleans as a flatboat hand, temporarily joining a trade many members of which at that time still took pride in being called "half horse and half alligator." After his return he worked and lived in the old way until the spring of 1830, when his father "moved again," this time to Illinois; and on the journey of fifteen days "Abe" had to drive the ox wagon which carried the household goods. Another log cabin was built, and then, fencing a field, Abraham Lincoln split those historic rails which were destined to play so picturesque a part in the presidential campaign twenty-eight years later.

Having come of age, Lincoln left the family, and "struck out for himself." He had to "take jobs whenever he could get them." The first of these carried him again as a flatboat hand to New Orleans. There something happened that made a lasting impression upon his soul: he witnessed a slave auction. "His heart bled," wrote one of his companions; "said nothing much; was silent; looked bad. I can say, knowing it, that it was on this trip that he formed his opinion on slavery. It run its iron in him then and there, May, 1831. I have heard him say so often." Then he lived several years at New Salem, in Illinois, a small mushroom village, with a mill, some "stores" and whiskey shops, that rose quickly, and soon disappeared again. It was a desolate, disjointed, half-working, and half-loitering life, without any other aim than to gain food and shelter from day to day. He served as pilot on a steamboat trip, then as clerk in a. store and a mill; business failing, he was adrift for some time. Being compelled to measure his strength with the chief bully of the neighborhood, and overcoming him, he became a noted person in that muscular community, and won the esteem and friendship of the ruling gang of ruffians to such a degree that, when the Black Hawk war[Footnote 1: Black Hawk was a chief of the Indian tribe of Sacs. The Sacs and Foxes made a treaty in 1830, by which their lands in Illinois were ceded to the United States, and the Indians were to remove beyond the Mississippi. Black Hawk refused submission, and in 1832 appeared with a thousand men; but a force was raised in Illinois which destroyed, dispersed, or made captive the whole body.—ED.] broke out, they elected him, a young man of twenty-three, captain of a volunteer company, composed mainly of roughs of their kind. He took the field, and his most noteworthy deed of valor consisted, not in killing an Indian, but in protecting against his own men, at the peril of his own life, the life of an old savage who had strayed into his camp.

The Black Hawk war over, he turned to politics. The step from the captaincy of a volunteer company to a candidacy for a seat in the legislature seemed a natural one. But his popularity, although great in New Salem, had not spread far enough over the district, and he was defeated. Then the wretched hand-to-mouth struggle began again. He "set up in store business" with a dissolute partner, who drank whiskey while Lincoln was reading books. The result was a disastrous failure and a load of debt. Thereupon he became a deputy surveyor, and was appointed postmaster of New Salem, the business of the post-office being so small that he could carry the incoming and outgoing mail in his hat. All this could not lift him from poverty, and his surveying instruments and horse and saddle were sold by the sheriff for debt.

But while all this misery was upon him, his ambition rose to higher aims. He walked many miles to borrow from a schoolmaster a grammar with which to improve his language. A lawyer lent him a copy of Blackstone, and he began to study law. People would look wonderingly at the grotesque figure lying in the grass, "with his feet up a tree," or sitting on a fence, as, absorbed in a book, he learned to construct correct sentences and made himself a jurist. At once he gained a little practice, pettifogging before a justice of the peace for friends, without expecting a fee. Judicial functions, too, were thrust upon him, but only at horse-races or wrestling matches, where his acknowledged honesty and fairness gave his verdicts undisputed authority. His popularity grew apace, and soon he could be a candidate for the legislature again. Although he called himself a Whig, an ardent admirer of Henry Clay, his clever stump speeches won him the election in the strongly Democratic district. Then for the first time, perhaps, he thought seriously of his outward appearance. So far he had been content with a garb of "Kentucky jeans," not seldom ragged, usually patched, and always shabby. Now he borrowed some money from a friend to buy a new suit of clothes—"store clothes"—fit for a Sangamon County statesman; and thus adorned he set out for the state capital, Vandalia, to take his seat among the lawmakers.

His legislative career, which stretched over several sessions, for he was thrice reelected, in 1836, 1838, and 1840, was not remarkably brilliant. He did, indeed, not lack ambition. He dreamed even of making himself "the De Witt Clinton of Illinois," and he actually distinguished himself by zealous and effective work in those "log-rolling" operations by which the young State received "a general system of internal improvements" in the shape of railroads, canals, and banks,—a reckless policy, burdening the State with debt, and producing the usual crop of political demoralization, but a policy characteristic of the time and the impatiently enterprising spirit of the Western people. Lincoln, no doubt with the best intentions, but with little knowledge of the subject, simply followed the popular current. The achievement in which, perhaps, he gloried most was the removal of the state government from Vandalia to Springfield,—one of those triumphs of political management which are apt to be the pride of the small politician's statesmanship. One thing, however, he did in which his true nature asserted itself, and which gave distinct promise of the future pursuit of high aims. Against an overwhelming preponderance of sentiment in the legislature, followed by only one other member, he recorded his protest against a proslavery resolution,—that protest declaring "the institution of slavery to be founded on both injustice and bad policy." This was not only the irrepressible voice of his conscience; it was true moral valor, too; for at that time, in many parts of the West, an abolitionist was regarded as little better than a horse-thief, and even "Abe Lincoln" would hardly have been forgiven his anti-slavery principles, had he not been known as such an "uncommon good fellow." But here, in obedience to the great conviction of his life, he manifested his courage to stand alone,—that courage which is the first requisite of leadership in a great cause.

Together with his reputation and influence as a politician grew his law practice, especially after he had removed from New Salem to Springfield, and associated himself with a practitioner of good standing. He had now at last won a fixed position in society. He became a successful lawyer, less, indeed, by his learning as a jurist than by his effectiveness as an advocate and by the striking uprightness of his character; and it may truly be said that his vivid sense of truth and justice had much to do with his effectiveness as an advocate. He would refuse to act as the attorney even of personal friends when he saw the right on the other side. He would abandon cases, even during trial, when the testimony convinced him that his client was in the wrong. He would dissuade those who sought his service from pursuing an obtainable advantage when their claims seemed to him unfair. Presenting his very first case in the United States Circuit Court, the only question being one of authority, he declared that, upon careful examination, he found all the authorities on the other side, and none on his. Persons accused of crime, when he thought them guilty, he would not defend at all, or, attempting their defence, he was unable to put forth his powers. One notable exception is on record, when his personal sympathies had been strongly aroused. But when he felt himself to be the protector of innocence, the defender of justice, or the prosecutor of wrong, he frequently disclosed such unexpected resources of reasoning, such depth of feeling, and rose to such fervor of appeal as to astonish and overwhelm his hearers and make him fairly irresistible. Even an ordinary law argument, coming from him, seldom failed to produce the impression that he was profoundly convinced of the soundness of his position. It is not surprising that the mere appearance of so conscientious an attorney in any case should have carried, not only to juries, but even to judges, almost a presumption of right on his side, and that the people began to call him, sincerely meaning it, "honest Abe Lincoln."

In the mean time he had private sorrows and trials of a painfully afflicting nature. He had loved and been loved by a fair and estimable girl, Ann Rutledge, who died in the flower of her youth and beauty, and he mourned her loss with such intensity of grief that his friends feared for his reason. Recovering from his morbid depression, he bestowed what he thought a new affection upon another lady, who refused him. And finally, moderately prosperous in his worldly affairs, and having prospects of political distinction before him, he paid his addresses to Mary Todd, of Kentucky, and was accepted. But then tormenting doubts of the genuineness of his own affection for her, of the compatibility of their characters, and of their future happiness came upon him. His distress was so great that he felt himself in danger of suicide, and feared to carry a pocket-knife with him; and he gave mortal offence to his bride by not appearing on the appointed wedding day. Now the torturing consciousness of the wrong he had done her grew unendurable. He won back her affection, ended the agony by marrying her, and became a faithful and patient husband and a good father. But it was no secret, to those who knew the family well, that his domestic life was full of trials. The erratic temper of his wife not seldom put the gentleness of his nature to the severest tests; and these troubles and struggles, which accompanied him through all the vicissitudes of his life from the modest home in Springfield to the White House at Washington, adding untold private heartburnings to his public cares, and sometimes precipitating upon him incredible embarrassments in the discharge of his public duties, form one of the most pathetic features of his career.

He continued to "ride the circuit," read books while travelling in his buggy, told funny stories to his fellow lawyers in the tavern, chatted familiarly with his neighbors around the stove in the store and at the post-office, had his hours of melancholy brooding as of old, and became more and more widely known and trusted and beloved among the people of his State for his ability as a lawyer and politician, for the uprightness of his character and the ever-flowing spring of sympathetic kindness in his heart. His main ambition was confessedly that of political distinction; but hardly any one would at that time have seen in him the man destined to lead the nation through the greatest crisis of the century.

His time had not yet come when, in 1846, he was elected to Congress. In a clever speech in the House of Representatives, he denounced President Polk for having unjustly forced war upon Mexico, and he amused the Committee of the Whole by a witty attack upon General Cass. More important was the expression he gave to his anti-slavery impulses by offering a bill looking to the emancipation of the slaves in the District of Columbia, and by his repeated votes for the famous Wilmot Proviso, intended to exclude slavery from the Territories acquired from Mexico. But when, at the expiration of his term, in March, 1849, he left his seat, he gloomily despaired of ever seeing the day when the cause nearest to his heart would be rightly grasped by the people, and when he would be able to render any service to his country in solving the great problem. Nor had his career as a member of Congress in any sense been such as to gratify his ambition. Indeed, if he ever had any belief in a great destiny for himself, it must have been weak at that period; for he actually sought to obtain from the new Whig President, General Taylor, the place of Commissioner of the General Land Office, willing to bury himself in one of the administrative bureaus of the government. Fortunately for the country, he failed; and no less fortunately, when, later, the territorial governorship of Oregon was offered to him, Mrs. Lincoln's protest induced him to decline it. Returning to Springfield, he gave himself with renewed zest to his law practice, acquiesced in the Compromise of 1850 with reluctance and a mental reservation, supported in the presidential campaign of 1852 the Whig candidate in some spiritless speeches, and took but a languid interest in the politics of the day. But just then his time was drawing near.

The peace promised, and apparently inaugurated, by the Compromise of 1850 was rudely broken by the introduction of the Kansas-Nebraska bill in 1854. The repeal of the Missouri Compromise, opening the Territories of the United States, the heritage of coming generations, to the invasion of slavery, suddenly revealed the whole significance of the slavery question to the people of the free States, and thrust itself into the politics of the country as the paramount issue. Something like an electric shock flashed through the North. Men who but a short time before had been absorbed by their business pursuits, and deprecated all political agitation, were startled out of their security by a sudden alarm, and excitedly took sides. That restless trouble of conscience about slavery, which even in times of apparent repose had secretly disturbed the souls of Northern people, broke forth in an utterance louder than ever. The bonds of accustomed party allegiance gave way. Anti-slavery Democrats and anti-slavery Whigs felt themselves drawn together by a common overpowering sentiment, and soon they began to rally in a new organization. The Republican party sprang into being to meet the overruling call of the hour. Then Abraham Lincoln's time was come. He rapidly advanced to a position of conspicuous championship in the struggle. This, however, was not owing to his virtues and abilities alone. Indeed, the slavery question stirred his soul in its profoundest depths; it was, as one of his intimate friends said, "the only one on which he would become excited;" it called forth all his faculties and energies. Yet there were many others who, having long and arduously fought the anti-slavery battle in the popular assembly, or in the press, or in the halls of Congress, far surpassed him in prestige, and compared with whom he was still an obscure and untried man. His reputation, although highly honorable and well earned, had so far been essentially local. As a stump-speaker in Whig canvasses outside of his State, he had attracted comparatively little attention; but in Illinois he had been recognized as one of the foremost men of the Whig party. Among the opponents of the Nebraska bill he occupied in his State so important a position, that in 1854 he was the choice of a large majority of the "Anti-Nebraska men" in the legislature for a seat in the Senate of the United States which then became vacant; and when he, an old Whig, could not obtain the votes of the Anti-Nebraska Democrats necessary to make a majority, he generously urged his friends to transfer their votes to Lyman Trumbull, who was then elected. Two years later, in the first national convention of the Republican party, the delegation from Illinois brought him forward as a candidate for the vice-presidency, and he received respectable support. Still, the name of Abraham Lincoln was not widely known beyond the boundaries of his own State. But now it was this local prominence in Illinois that put him in a position of peculiar advantage on the battlefield of national politics. In the assault on the Missouri Compromise which broke down all legal barriers to the spread of slavery, Stephen Arnold Douglas was the ostensible leader and central figure; and Douglas was a senator from Illinois, Lincoln's State. Douglas's national theatre of action was the Senate, but in his constituency in Illinois were the roots of his official position and power. What he did in the Senate he had to justify before the people of Illinois, in order to maintain himself in place; and in Illinois all eyes turned to Lincoln as Douglas's natural antagonist.

As very young men they had come to Illinois, Lincoln from Indiana, Douglas from Vermont, and had grown up together in public life, Douglas as a Democrat, Lincoln as a Whig. They had met first in Vandalia, in 1834, when Lincoln was in the legislature and Douglas in the lobby; and again in 1836, both as members of the legislature. Douglas, a very able politician, of the agile, combative, audacious, "pushing" sort, rose in political distinction with remarkable rapidity. In quick succession he became a member of the legislature, a State's attorney, Secretary of State, a judge on the supreme bench of Illinois, three times a representative in Congress, and a senator of the United States when only thirty-nine years old. In the national Democratic convention of 1852, he appeared even as an aspirant to the nomination for the presidency, as the favorite of "young America," and received a respectable vote. He had far outstripped Lincoln in what is commonly called political success and in reputation. But it had frequently happened that in political campaigns Lincoln felt himself impelled, or was selected by his Whig friends, to answer Douglas's speeches; and thus the two were looked upon, in a large part of the State at least, as the representative combatants of their respective parties in the debates before popular meetings. As soon, therefore, as, after the passage of his Kansas-Nebraska bill, Douglas returned to Illinois to defend his cause before his constituents, Lincoln, obeying not 'only his own impulse, but also general expectation, stepped forward as his principal opponent. Thus the struggle about the principles involved in the Kansas-Nebraska bill, or, in a broader sense, the struggle between freedom and slavery, assumed in Illinois the outward form of a personal contest between Lincoln and Douglas; and as it continued and became more animated, that personal contest in Illinois was watched with constantly increasing interest by the whole country. When, in 1858, Douglas's senatorial term being about to expire, Lincoln was formally designated by the Republican convention of Illinois as their candidate for the Senate, to take Douglas's place, and the two contestants agreed to debate the questions at issue face to face in a series of public meetings, the eyes of the whole American people were turned eagerly to that one point; and the spectacle reminded one of those lays of ancient times telling of two armies, in battle array, standing still to see their two principal champions fight out the contested cause between the lines in single combat.

Lincoln had then reached the full maturity of his powers. His equipment as a statesman did not embrace a comprehensive knowledge of public affairs. What he had studied he had indeed made his own, with the eager craving and that zealous tenacity characteristic of superior minds learning under difficulties. But his narrow opportunities and the unsteady life he had led during his younger years had not permitted the accumulation of large stores in his mind. It is true, in political campaigns he had occasionally spoken on the ostensible issues between the Whigs and the Democrats, the tariff, internal improvements, banks, and so on, but only in a perfunctory manner. Had he ever given much serious thought and study to these subjects, it is safe to assume that a mind so prolific of original conceits as his would certainly have produced some utterance upon them worth remembering. His soul had evidently never been deeply stirred by such topics. But when his moral nature was aroused, his brain developed an untiring activity until it had mastered all the knowledge within reach. As soon as the repeal of the Missouri Compromise had thrust the slavery question into politics as the paramount issue, Lincoln plunged into an arduous study of all its legal, historical, and moral aspects, and then his mind became a complete arsenal of argument. His rich natural gifts, trained by long and varied practice, had made him an orator of rare persuasiveness. In his immature days, he had pleased himself for a short period with that inflated, high-flown style which, among the uncultivated, passes for "beautiful speaking." His inborn truthfulness and his artistic instinct soon overcame that aberration, and revealed to him the noble beauty and strength of simplicity. He possessed an uncommon power of clear and compact statement, which might have reminded those who knew the story of his early youth of the efforts of the poor boy, when he copied his compositions from the scraped wooden shovel, carefully to trim his expressions in order to save paper. His language had the energy of honest directness, and he was a master of logical lucidity. He loved to point and enliven his reasoning by humorous illustrations, usually anecdotes of Western life, of which he had an inexhaustible store at his command. These anecdotes had not seldom a flavor of rustic robustness about them, but he used them with great effect, while amusing the audience, to give life to an abstraction, to explode an absurdity, to clinch an argument, to drive home an admonition. The natural kindliness of his tone, softening prejudice and disarming partisan rancor, would often open to his reasoning a way into minds most unwilling to receive it.

Yet his greatest power consisted in the charm of his individuality. That charm did not, in the ordinary way, appeal to the ear or to the eye. His voice was not melodious; rather shrill and piercing, especially when it rose to its high treble in moments of great animation. His figure was unhandsome, and the action of his unwieldy limbs awkward. He commanded none of the outward graces of oratory as they are commonly understood. His charm was of a different kind. It flowed from the rare depth and genuineness of his convictions and his sympathetic feelings. Sympathy was the strongest element in his nature. One of his biographers, who knew him before he became President, says: "Lincoln's compassion might be stirred deeply by an object present, but never by an object absent and unseen. In the former case he would most likely extend relief, with little inquiry into the merits of the case, because, as he expressed it himself, it 'took a pain out of his own heart.'" Only half of this is correct. It is certainly true that he could not witness any individual distress or oppression, or any kind of suffering, without feeling a pang of pain himself, and that by relieving as much as he could the suffering of others he put an end to his own. This compassionate impulse to help he felt not only for human beings, but for every living creature. As in his boyhood he angrily reproved the boys who tormented a wood turtle by putting a burning coal on its back, so, we are told, he would, when a mature man, on a journey, dismount from his buggy and wade waist-deep in mire to rescue a pig struggling in a swamp. Indeed, appeals to his compassion were so irresistible to him, and he felt it so difficult to refuse anything when his refusal could give pain, that he himself sometimes spoke of his inability to say "no" as a positive weakness. But that certainly does not prove that his compassionate feeling was confined to individual cases of suffering witnessed with his own eyes. As the boy was moved by the aspect of the tortured wood turtle to compose an essay against cruelty to animals in general, so the aspect of other cases of suffering and wrong wrought up his moral nature, and set his mind to work against cruelty, injustice, and oppression in general.

As his sympathy went forth to others, it attracted others to him. Especially those whom he called the "plain people" felt themselves drawn to him by the instinctive feeling that he understood, esteemed, and appreciated them. He had grown up among the poor, the lowly, the ignorant. He never ceased to remember the good souls he had met among them, and the many kindnesses they had done him. Although in his mental development he had risen far above them, he never looked down upon them. How they felt and how they reasoned he knew, for so he had once felt and reasoned himself. How they could be moved he knew, for so he had once been moved himself, and he practised moving others. His mind was much larger than theirs, but it thoroughly comprehended theirs; and while he thought much farther than they, their thoughts were ever present to him. Nor had the visible distance between them grown as wide as his rise in the world would seem to have warranted. Much of his backwoods speech and manners still clung to him. Although he had become "Mr. Lincoln" to his later acquaintances, he was still "Abe" to the "Nats" and "Billys" and "Daves" of his youth; and their familiarity neither appeared unnatural to them, nor was it in the least awkward to him. He still told and enjoyed stories similar to those he had told and enjoyed in the Indiana settlement and at New Salem. His wants remained as modest as they had ever been; his domestic habits had by no means completely accommodated themselves to those of his more high-born wife; and though the "Kentucky jeans" apparel had long been dropped, his clothes of better material and better make would sit ill sorted on his gigantic limbs. His cotton umbrella, without a handle, and tied together with a coarse string to keep it from flapping, when he carried on his circuit rides, is said to be remembered still by some of his surviving neighbors. This rusticity of habit was utterly free from that affected contempt of refinement and comfort which self-made men sometimes carry into their more affluent circumstances. To Abraham Lincoln it was entirely natural, and all those who came into contact with him knew it to be so. In his ways of thinking and feeling he had become a gentleman in the highest sense, but the refining process had polished but little the outward form. The plain people, therefore, still considered "honest Abe Lincoln" one of themselves: and when they felt, which they no doubt frequently did, that his thoughts and aspirations moved in a sphere above their own, they were all the more proud of him, without any diminution of fellow feeling. It was this relation of mutual sympathy and understanding between Lincoln and the plain people that gave him his peculiar power as a public man, and singularly fitted him, as we shall see, for that leadership which was preeminently required in the great crisis then coming on,—the leadership which indeed thinks and moves ahead of the masses, but always remains within sight and sympathetic touch of them.

He entered upon the campaign of 1858 better equipped than he had ever been before. He not only instinctively felt, but he had convinced himself by arduous study, that in this struggle against the spread of slavery he had right, justice, philosophy, the enlightened opinion of mankind, history, the Constitution, and good policy on his side. It was observed that after he began to discuss the slavery question his speeches were pitched in a much loftier key than his former oratorical efforts. While he remained fond of telling funny stories in private conversation, they disappeared more and more from his public discourse. He would still now and then point his argument with expressions of inimitable quaintness, and flash out rays of kindly humor and witty irony; but his general tone was serious, and rose sometimes to genuine solemnity. His masterly skill in dialectical thrust and parry, his wealth of knowledge, his power of reasoning, and elevation of sentiment, disclosed in language of rare precision, strength, and beauty, not seldom astonished his old friends.

Neither of the two champions could have found a more formidable antagonist than each now met in the other. Douglas was by far the most conspicuous member of his party. His admirers had dubbed him "the little giant," contrasting in that nickname the greatness of his mind with the smallness of his body. But though of low stature, his broad-shouldered figure appeared uncommonly sturdy, and there was something lion-like in the squareness of his brow and jaw, and in the defiant shake of his long hair. His loud and persistent advocacy of territorial expansion, in the name of patriotism and "manifest destiny," had given him an enthusiastic following among the young and ardent. Great natural parts, a highly combative temperament, and long training had made him a debater unsurpassed in a Senate filled with able men. He could be as forceful in his appeals to patriotic feelings as he was fierce in denunciation and thoroughly skilled in all the baser tricks of parliamentary pugilism. While genial and rollicking in his social intercourse,—the idol of the "boys,"—he felt himself one of the most renowned statesmen of his time, and would frequently meet his opponents with an overbearing haughtiness, as persons more to be pitied than to be feared. In his speech opening the campaign of 1858, he spoke of Lincoln, whom the Republicans had dared to advance as their candidate for "his" place in the Senate, with an air of patronizing if not contemptuous condescension, as "a kind, amiable, and intelligent gentleman and a good citizen." The little giant would have been pleased to pass off his antagonist as a tall dwarf. He knew Lincoln too well, however, to indulge himself seriously in such a delusion. But the political situation was at that moment in a curious tangle, and Douglas could expect to derive from the confusion great advantage over his opponent.

By the repeal of the Missouri Compromise, opening the Territories to the ingress of slavery, Douglas had pleased the South, but greatly alarmed the North. He had sought to conciliate Northern sentiment by appending to his Kansas-Nebraska bill the declaration that its intent was "not to legislate slavery into any State or Territory, nor to exclude it therefrom, but to leave the people thereof perfectly free to form and regulate their institutions in their own way, subject only to the Constitution of the United States." This he called "the great principle of popular sovereignty." When asked whether, under this act, the people of a Territory, before its admission as a State, would have the right to exclude slavery, he answered, "That is a question for the courts to decide." Then came the famous "Dred Scott decision," in which the Supreme Court held substantially that the right to hold slaves as property existed in the Territories by virtue of the Federal Constitution, and that this right could not be denied by any act of a territorial government. This, of course, denied the right of the people of any Territory to exclude slavery while they were in a territorial condition, and it alarmed the Northern people still more. Douglas recognized the binding force of the decision of the Supreme Court, at the same time maintaining, most illogically, that his great principle of popular sovereignty remained in force nevertheless. Meanwhile, the pro-slavery people of western Missouri, the so-called "border ruffians," had invaded Kansas, set up a constitutional convention, made a constitution of an extreme pro-slavery type, the "Lecompton Constitution," refused to submit it fairly to a vote of the people of Kansas, and then referred it to Congress for acceptance,—seeking thus to accomplish the admission of Kansas as a slave State. Had Douglas supported such a scheme, he would have lost all foothold in the North. In the name of popular sovereignty he loudly declared his opposition to the acceptance of any constitution not sanctioned by a formal popular vote. He "did not care," he said, "whether slavery be voted up or down," but there must be a fair vote of the people. Thus he drew upon himself the hostility of the Buchanan administration, which was controlled by the pro-slavery interest, but he saved his Northern following. More than this, not only did his Democratic admirers now call him "the true champion of freedom," but even some Republicans of large influence, prominent among them Horace Greeley, sympathizing with Douglas in his fight against the Lecompton Constitution, and hoping to detach him permanently from the pro-slavery interest and to force a lasting breach in the Democratic party, seriously advised the Republicans of Illinois to give up their opposition to Douglas, and to help reelect him to the Senate. Lincoln was not of that opinion. He believed that great popular movements can succeed only when guided by their faithful friends, and that the anti-slavery cause could not safely be intrusted to the keeping of one who "did not care whether slavery be voted up or down." This opinion prevailed in Illinois; but the influences within the Republican party, over which it prevailed, yielded only a reluctant acquiescence, if they acquiesced at all, after having materially strengthened Douglas's position. Such was the situation of things when the campaign of 1858 between Lincoln and Douglas began.

Lincoln opened the campaign on his side, at the convention which nominated him as the Republican candidate for the senatorship, with a memorable saying which sounded like a shout from the watch-tower of history: "A house divided against itself cannot stand. I believe this government cannot endure permanently half slave and half free. I do not expect the Union to be dissolved. I do not expect the house to fall, but I expect it will cease to be divided. It will become all one thing or all the other. Either the opponents of slavery will arrest the further spread of it, and place it where the public mind shall rest in the belief that it is in the course of ultimate extinction; or its advocates will push it forward, till it shall become alike lawful in all the States,—old as well as new, North as well as South." Then he proceeded to point out that the Nebraska doctrine combined with the Dred Scott decision worked in the direction of making the nation "all slave." Here was the "irrepressible conflict" spoken of by Seward a short time later, in a speech made famous mainly by that phrase. If there was any new discovery in it, the right of priority was Lincoln's. This utterance proved not only his statesmanlike conception of the issue, but also, in his situation as a candidate, the firmness of his moral courage. The friends to whom he had read the draught of this speech before he delivered it warned him anxiously that its delivery might be fatal to his success in the election. This was shrewd advice, in the ordinary sense. While a slaveholder could threaten disunion with impunity, the mere suggestion that the existence of slavery was incompatible with freedom in the Union would hazard the political chances of any public man in the North. But Lincoln was inflexible. "It is true," said he, "and I ***will*** deliver it as written. . . . I would rather be defeated with these expressions in my speech held up and discussed before the people than be victorious without them." The statesman was right in his far-seeing judgment and his conscientious statement of the truth, but the practical politicians were also right in their prediction of the immediate effect. Douglas instantly seized upon the declaration that a house divided against itself cannot stand as the main objective point of his attack, interpreting it as an incitement to a "relentless sectional war," and there is no doubt that the persistent reiteration of this charge served to frighten not a few timid souls.

Lincoln constantly endeavored to bring the moral and philosophical side of the subject to the foreground. "Slavery is wrong" was the keynote of all his speeches. To Douglas's glittering sophism that the right of the people of a Territory to have slavery or not, as they might desire, was in accordance with the principle of true popular sovereignty, he made the pointed answer: "Then true popular sovereignty, according to Senator Douglas, means that, when one man makes another man his slave, no third man shall be allowed to object." To Douglas's argument that the principle which demanded that the people of a Territory should be permitted to choose whether they would have slavery or not "originated when God made man, and placed good and evil before him, allowing him to choose upon his own responsibility," Lincoln solemnly replied: "No; God did not place good and evil before man, telling him to make his choice. On the contrary, God did tell him there was one tree of the fruit of which he should not eat, upon pain of death." He did not, however, place himself on the most advanced ground taken by the radical anti-slavery men. He admitted that, under the Constitution, "the Southern people were entitled to a congressional fugitive slave law," although he did not approve the fugitive slave law then existing. He declared also that, if slavery were kept out of the Territories during their territorial existence, as it should be, and if then the people of any Territory, having a fair chance and a clear field, should do such an extraordinary thing as to adopt a slave constitution, uninfluenced by the actual presence of the institution among them, he saw no alternative but to admit such a Territory into the Union. He declared further that, while he should be exceedingly glad to see slavery abolished in the District of Columbia, he would, as a member of Congress, with his present views, not endeavor to bring on that abolition except on condition that emancipation be gradual, that it be approved by the decision of a majority of voters in the District, and that compensation be made to unwilling owners. On every available occasion, he pronounced himself in favor of the deportation and colonization of the blacks, of course with their consent. He repeatedly disavowed any wish on his part to have social and political equality established between whites and blacks. On this point he summed up his views in a reply to Douglas's assertion that the Declaration of Independence, in speaking of all men as being created equal, did not include the negroes, saying: "I do not understand the Declaration of Independence to mean that all men were created equal in all respects. They are not equal in color. But I believe that it does mean to declare that all men are equal in some respects; they are equal in their right to life, liberty, and the pursuit of happiness."

"With regard to some of these subjects Lincoln modified his position at a later period, and it has been suggested that he would have professed more advanced principles in his debates with Douglas, had he not feared thereby to lose votes. This view can hardly be sustained. Lincoln had the courage of his opinions, but he was not a radical. The man who risked his election by delivering, against the urgent protest of his friends, the speech about "the house divided against itself" would not have shrunk from the expression of more extreme views, had he really entertained them. It is only fair to assume that he said what at the time he really thought, and that if, subsequently, his opinions changed, it was owing to new conceptions of good policy and of duty brought forth by an entirely new set of circumstances and exigencies. It is characteristic that he continued to adhere to the impracticable colonization plan even after the Emancipation Proclamation had already been issued.

But in this contest Lincoln proved himself not only a debater, but also a political strategist of the first order. The "kind, amiable, and intelligent gentleman," as Douglas had been pleased to call him, was by no means as harmless as a dove. He possessed an uncommon share of that worldly shrewdness which not seldom goes with genuine simplicity of character; and the political experience gathered in the legislature and in Congress and in many election campaigns, added to his keen intuitions, had made him as far-sighted a judge of the probable effects of a public man's sayings or doings upon the popular mind, and as accurate a calculator in estimating political chances and forecasting results, as could be found among the party managers in Illinois. And now he perceived keenly the ugly dilemma in which Douglas found himself, between the Dred Scott decision, which declared the right to hold slaves to exist in the Territories by virtue of the Federal Constitution, and his "great principle of popular sovereignty," according to which the people of a Territory, if they saw fit, were to have the right to exclude slavery therefrom. Douglas was twisting and squirming to the best of his ability to avoid the admission that the two were incompatible. The question then presented itself if it would be good policy for Lincoln to force Douglas to a clear expression of his opinion as to whether, the Dred Scott decision notwithstanding, "the people of a Territory could in any lawful way exclude slavery from its limits prior to the formation of a state constitution." Lincoln foresaw and predicted what Douglas would answer: that slavery could not exist in a Territory unless the people desired it and gave it protection by territorial legislation. In an improvised caucus the policy of pressing the interrogatory on Douglas was discussed. Lincoln's friends unanimously advised against it, because the answer foreseen would sufficiently commend Douglas to the people of Illinois to insure his reëlection to the Senate. But Lincoln persisted. "I am after larger game," said he. "If Douglas so answers, he can never be President, and the battle of 1860 is worth a hundred of this." The interrogatory was pressed upon Douglas, and Douglas did answer that, no matter what the decision of the Supreme Court might be on the abstract question, the people of a Territory had the lawful means to introduce or exclude slavery by territorial legislation friendly or unfriendly to the institution. Lincoln found it easy to show the absurdity of the proposition that, if slavery were admitted to exist of right in the Territories by virtue of the supreme law, the Federal Constitution, it could be kept out or expelled by an inferior law, one made by a territorial legislature. Again the judgment of the politicians, having only the nearest object in view, proved correct: Douglas was reëlected to the Senate. But Lincoln's judgment proved correct also: Douglas, by resorting to the expedient of his "unfriendly legislation doctrine," forfeited his last chance of becoming President of the United States. He might have hoped to win, by sufficient atonement, his pardon from the South for his opposition to the Lecompton Constitution; but that he taught the people of the Territories a trick by which they could defeat what the pro-slavery men considered a constitutional right, and that he called that trick lawful,—this the slave power would never forgive. The breach between the Southern and the Northern democracy was thenceforth irremediable and fatal.

The presidential election of 1860 approached. The struggle in Kansas, and the debates in Congress which accompanied it, and which not unfrequently provoked violent outbursts, continually stirred the popular excitement. Within the Democratic party raged the war of factions. The national Democratic convention met at Charleston on the 23d of April, 1860. After a struggle of ten days between the adherents and the opponents of Douglas, during which the delegates from the cotton States had withdrawn, the convention adjourned without having nominated any candidates, to meet again in Baltimore on the 18th of June. There was no prospect, however, of reconciling the hostile elements. It appeared very probable that the Baltimore convention would nominate Douglas, while the seceding Southern Democrats would set up a candidate of their own, representing extreme pro-slavery principles.

Meanwhile, the national Republican convention assembled at Chicago on the 16th of May, full of enthusiasm and hope. The situation was easily understood. The

Democrats would have the South. In order to succeed in the election, the Republicans had to win, in addition to the States carried by Frémont in 1856, those that were classed as "doubtful,"—New Jersey, Pennsylvania, and Indiana, or Illinois in the place of either New Jersey or Indiana. The most eminent Republican statesmen and leaders of the time thought of for the presidency were Seward and Chase, both regarded as belonging to the more advanced order of anti-slavery men. Of the two, Seward had the largest following, mainly from New York, New England, and the Northwest. Cautious politicians doubted seriously whether Seward, to whom some phrases in his speeches had undeservedly given the reputation of a reckless radical, would be able to command the whole Republican vote in the doubtful States. Besides, during his long public career he had made enemies. It was evident that those who thought Seward's nomination too hazardous an experiment would consider Chase unavailable for the same reason. They would then look round for an "available" man; and among the "available" men Abraham Lincoln was easily discovered to stand foremost. His great debate with Douglas had given him a national reputation. The people of the East being eager to see the hero of so dramatic a contest, he had been induced to visit several Eastern cities, and had astonished and delighted large and distinguished audiences with speeches of singular power and originality. An address delivered by him in the Cooper Institute in New York, before an audience containing a large number of important persons, was then, and has ever since been, especially praised as one of the most logical and convincing political speeches ever made in this country. The people of the West had grown proud of him as a distinctively Western great man, and his popularity at home had some peculiar features which could be expected to exercise a potent charm. Nor was Lincoln's name as that of an available candidate left to the chance of accidental discovery. It is indeed not probable that he thought of himself as a presidential possibility, during his contest with Douglas for the senatorship. As late as April, 1859, he had written to a friend who had approached him on the subject that he did not think himself fit for the presidency. The vice-presidency was then the limit of his ambition. But some of his friends in Illinois took the matter seriously in hand, and Lincoln, after some hesitation, then formally authorized "the use of his name." The matter was managed with such energy and excellent judgment that in the convention he had not only the whole vote of Illinois to start with, but won votes on all sides without offending any rival. A large majority of the opponents of Seward went over to Abraham Lincoln, and gave him the nomination on the third ballot. As had been foreseen, Douglas was nominated by one wing of the Democratic party at Baltimore, while the extreme pro-slavery wing put Breckinridge into the field as its candidate. After a campaign conducted with the energy of genuine enthusiasm on the anti-slavery side, the united Republicans defeated the divided Democrats, and Lincoln was elected President by a majority of fifty-seven votes in the electoral colleges.

The result of the election had hardly been declared when the disunion movement in the South, long threatened and carefully planned and prepared, broke out in the shape of open revolt, and nearly a month before Lincoln could be inaugurated as President of the United States, seven Southern States had adopted ordinances of secession, formed an independent confederacy, framed a constitution for it, and elected Jefferson Davis its president, expecting the other slaveholding States soon to join them. On the 11th of February, 1861, Lincoln left Springfield for Washington; having, with characteristic simplicity, asked his law partner not to change the sign of the firm "Lincoln and Herndon" during the four years' unavoidable absence of the senior partner, and having taken an affectionate and touching; leave of his neighbors.

The situation which confronted the new President was appalling: the larger part of the South in open rebellion, the rest of the slaveholding States wavering, preparing to follow; the revolt guided by determined, daring, and skilful leaders; the Southern people, apparently full of enthusiasm and military spirit, rushing to arms, some of the forts and arsenals already in their possession; the government of the Union, before the accession of the new President, in the hands of men some of whom actively sympathized with the revolt, while others were hampered by their traditional doctrines in dealing with it, and really gave it aid and comfort by their irresolute attitude; all the departments full of "Southern sympathizers" and honeycombed with disloyalty; the treasury empty, and the public credit at the lowest ebb; the arsenals ill supplied with arms, if not emptied by treacherous practices; the regular army of insignificant strength, dispersed over an immense surface, and deprived by defection of some of its best officers; the navy small and antiquated. But that was not all. The threat of disunion had so often been resorted to by the slave power in years gone by that most Northern people had ceased to believe in its seriousness. But when disunion actually appeared as a stern reality, something like a chill swept through the whole Northern country. A cry for union and peace at any price rose on all sides. Democratic partisanship reiterated this cry with vociferous vehemence, and even many Republicans grew afraid of the victory they had just achieved at the ballot-box, and spoke of compromise. The country fairly resounded with the noise of "anticoercion meetings." Expressions of firm resolution from determined anti-slavery men were indeed not wanting, but they were for a while almost drowned by a bewildering confusion of discordant voices. Even this was not all. Potent influences in Europe, with an ill-concealed desire for the permanent disruption of the American Union, eagerly espoused the cause of the Southern seceders, and the two principal maritime powers of the Old World seemed only to be waiting for a favorable opportunity to lend them a helping hand.

This was the state of things to be mastered by "honest Abe Lincoln" when he took his seat in the presidential chair,—" honest Abe Lincoln," who was" so good natured that he could not say " no;" the greatest achievement in whose life had been a debate on the slavery question; who had never been in any position of power; who was without the slightest experience of high executive duties, and who had only a speaking acquaintance with the men upon whose counsel and cooperation he was to depend. Nor was his accession to power under such circumstances greeted with general confidence even by the members of his party. While he had indeed won much popularity, many Republicans, especially among those who had advocated Seward's nomination for the presidency, with a feeling little short of dismay, saw the simple "Illinois lawyer" take the reins of government. The orators and journals of the opposition were ridiculing and lampooning him without measure. Many people actually wondered how such a man could dare to undertake a task which, as he himself had said to his neighbors in his parting speech, was "more difficult than that of Washington himself had been."

But Lincoln brought to that task, aside from other uncommon qualities, the first requisite,—an intuitive comprehension of its nature. While he did not indulge in the delusion that the Union could be maintained or restored without a conflict of arms, he could indeed not foresee all the problems he would have to solve. He instinctively understood, however, by what means that conflict would have to be conducted by the government of a democracy. He knew that the impending war, whether great or small, would not be like a foreign war, exciting a united national enthusiasm, but a civil war, likely to fan to uncommon heat the animosities of party even in the localities controlled by the government; that this war would have to be carried on, not by means of a ready-made machinery, ruled by an undisputed, absolute will, but by means to be furnished by the voluntary action of the people:—armies to be formed by voluntary enlistment; large sums of money to be raised by the people, through their representatives, voluntarily taxing themselves; trusts of extraordinary power to be voluntarily granted; and war measures, not seldom restricting the rights and liberties to which the citizen was accustomed, to be voluntarily accepted and submitted to by the people, or at least a large majority of them;—and that this would have to be kept up, not merely during a short period of enthusiastic excitement, but possibly through weary years of alternating success and disaster, hope and despondency. He knew that in order to steer this government by public opinion successfully through all the confusion created by the prejudices and doubts and differences of sentiment distracting the popular mind, and so to propitiate, inspire, mould, organize, unite, and guide the popular will that it might give forth all the means required for the performance of his great task, he would have to take into account all the influences strongly affecting the current of popular thought and feeling, and to direct while appearing to obey.

This was the kind of leadership he intuitively conceived to be needed when a free people were to be led forward en masse to overcome a great common danger under circumstances of appalling difficulty,—the leadership which does not dash ahead with brilliant daring, no matter who follows, but which is intent upon rallying all the available forces, gathering in the stragglers, closing up the column, so that the front may advance well supported. For this leadership Abraham Lincoln was admirably fitted,—better than any other American statesman of his day; for he understood the plain people, with all their loves and hates, their prejudices and their noble impulses, their weaknesses and their strength, as he understood himself, and his sympathetic nature was apt to draw their sympathy to him.

His inaugural address[Footnote 1: Printed in Number 32, Riverside Literature series.] foreshadowed his official course in characteristic manner. Although yielding nothing in point of principle, it was by no means a flaming anti-slavery manifesto, such as would have pleased the more ardent Republicans. It was rather the entreaty of a sorrowing father speaking to his wayward children. In the kindliest language he pointed out to the secessionists how ill-advised their attempt at disunion was, and why, for their own sakes, they should desist. Almost plaintively he told them that, while it was not *their* duty to destroy the Union, it was **his** sworn duty to preserve it; that the least he could do, under the obligations of his oath, was to possess and hold the property of the United States; that he hoped to do this peaceably; that he abhorred war for any purpose, and that they would have none unless they themselves were the aggressors. It was a masterpiece of persuasiveness; and while Lincoln had accepted many valuable amendments suggested by Seward, it was essentially his own. Probably Lincoln himself did not expect his inaugural address to have any effect upon the secessionists, for he must have known them to be resolved upon disunion at any cost. But it was an appeal to the wavering minds in the North, and upon them it made a profound impression. Every candid man, however timid and halting, had to admit that the President was bound by his oath to do his duty; that under that oath he could do no less than he said he would do; that if the secessionists resisted such an appeal as the President had made, they were bent upon mischief, and that the government must be supported against them. The partisan sympathy with the Southern insurrection which still existed in the North did indeed not disappear, but it diminished perceptibly under the influence of such reasoning. Those who still resisted it did so at the risk of appearing unpatriotic.

It must not be supposed, however, that Lincoln at once succeeded in pleasing everybody, even among his friends,—even among those nearest to him. In selecting his cabinet, which he did substantially before he left Springfield for Washington, he thought it wise to call to his assistance the strong men of his party, especially those who had given evidence of the support they commanded as his competitors in the Chicago convention. In them he found at the same time representatives of the different shades of opinion within the party, and of the different elements—former Whigs and former Democrats—from which the party had recruited itself. This was sound policy under the circumstances. It might indeed have been foreseen that among the members of a cabinet so composed, troublesome disagreements and rivalries would break out. But it was better for the President to have these strong and ambitious men near him as his coöperators than to have them as his critics in Congress, where their differences might have been composed in a common opposition to him. As members of his cabinet he could hope to control them, and to keep them busily employed in the service of a common purpose, if he had the strength to do so. Whether he did possess this strength was soon tested by a singularly rude trial.

There can be no doubt that the foremost members of his cabinet, Seward and Chase, the most eminent Republican statesmen, had felt themselves wronged by their party when in its national convention it preferred to them for the presidency a man whom, not unnaturally, they thought greatly their inferior in ability and experience as well as in service. The soreness of that disappointment was intensified when they saw this Western man in the White House, with so much of rustic manner and speech as still clung to him, meeting his fellow citizens, high and low, on a footing of equality, with the simplicity of his good nature unburdened by any conventional dignity of deportment, and dealing with the great business of state in an easy-going, unmethodical, and apparently somewhat irreverent way. They did not understand such a man. Especially Seward, who, as Secretary of State, considered himself next to the Chief Executive, and who quickly accustomed himself to giving orders and making arrangements upon his own motion, thought it necessary that he should rescue the direction of public affairs from hands so unskilled, and take full charge of them himself. At the end of the first month of the administration he submitted a "memorandum" to President Lincoln, which has been first brought to light by Nicolay and Hay,[Footnote 1: ***In their Life of Lincoln, in ten volumes, published by The Century Company, New York.***] and is one of their most valuable contributions to the history of those days. In that paper Seward actually told the President that, at the end of a month's administration, the government was still without a policy, either domestic or foreign; that the slavery question should be eliminated from the struggle about the Union; that the matter of the maintenance of the forts and other possessions in the South should be decided with that view; that explanations should be demanded categorically from the governments of Spain and France, which were then preparing, one for the annexation of San Domingo, and both for the invasion of Mexico; that if no satisfactory explanations were received war should be declared against Spain and France by the United States; that explanations should also be sought from Russia and Great Britain, and a vigorous continental spirit of independence against European intervention be aroused all over the American continent; that this policy should be incessantly pursued and directed by somebody; that either the President should devote himself entirely to it, or devolve the direction on some member of his cabinet, whereupon all debate on this policy must end.

This could be understood only as a formal demand that the President should acknowledge his own incompetency to perform his duties, content himself with the amusement of distributing post offices, and resign his power as to all important affairs into the hands of his Secretary of State. It seems to-day incomprehensible how a statesman of Seward's calibre could at that period conceive a plan of policy in which the slavery question had no place; a policy which rested upon the utterly delusive assumption that the secessionists, who had already formed their Southern Confederacy, and were with stern resolution preparing to fight for its independence, could be hoodwinked back into the Union by some sentimental demonstration against European interference; a policy which, at that critical moment, would have involved the Union in a foreign war, thus inviting foreign intervention in favor of the Southern Confederacy, and increasing tenfold its chances in the struggle for independence. But it is equally incomprehensible how Seward could fail to see that this demand of an unconditional surrender was a mortal insult to the head of the government, and that by putting his proposition on paper he delivered himself into the hands of the very man he had insulted; for had Lincoln, as most Presidents would have done, instantly dismissed Seward, and published the true reason for that dismissal, it would inevitably have been the end of Seward's career. But Lincoln did what not many of the noblest and greatest men in history would have been noble and great enough to do. He considered that Seward, if rightly controlled, was still capable of rendering great service to his country in the place in which he was. He ignored the insult, but firmly established his superiority. In his reply, which he forthwith dispatched, he told Seward that the administration had a domestic policy as laid down in the inaugural address with Seward's approval; that it had a foreign policy as traced in Seward's dispatches with the President's approval; that if any policy was to be maintained or changed, he, the President, was to direct that on his responsibility; and that in performing that duty the President had a right to the advice of his secretaries. Seward's fantastic schemes of foreign war and continental policies Lincoln brushed aside by passing them over in silence. Nothing more was said. Seward must have felt that he was at the mercy of a superior man; that his offensive proposition had been generously pardoned as a temporary aberration of a great mind, and that he could atone for it only by devoted personal loyalty. This he did. He was thoroughly subdued, and thenceforth submitted to Lincoln his dispatches for revision and amendment without a murmur. The war with European nations was no longer thought of; the slavery question found in due time its proper place in the struggle for the Union; and when, at a later period, the dismissal of Seward was demanded by dissatisfied senators who attributed to him the shortcomings of the administration, Lincoln stood stoutly by his faithful Secretary of State.

Chase, the Secretary of the Treasury, a man of superb presence, of eminent ability and ardent patriotism, of great natural dignity and a certain outward coldness of manner, which made him appear more difficult of approach than he really was, did not permit his disappointment to burst out in such extravagant demonstrations. But Lincoln's ways were so essentially different from his that they never became quite intelligible, and certainly not congenial to him. It might, perhaps, have been better had there been, at the beginning of the administration, some decided clash between Lincoln and Chase, as there was between Lincoln and Seward, to bring on a full mutual explanation, and to make Chase appreciate the real seriousness of Lincoln's nature. But as it was, their relations always remained somewhat formal, and Chase never felt quite at ease under a chief whom he could not understand, and whose character and powers he never learned to esteem at their true value. At the same time, he devoted himself zealously to the duties of his department, and did the country arduous service under circumstances of extreme difficulty. Nobody recognized this more heartily than Lincoln himself, and they managed to work together until near the end of Lincoln's first presidential term, when Chase, after some disagreements concerning appointments to office, resigned from the treasury; and after Taney's death, the President made him Chief Justice.

The rest of the cabinet consisted of men of less eminence, who subordinated themselves more easily. In January, 1862, Lincoln found it necessary to bow Cameron out of the war office, and to put in his place Edwin M. Stanton, a man of intensely practical mind, vehement impulses, fierce positiveness, ruthless energy, immense working power, lofty patriotism, and severest devotion to duty. He accepted the war office, not as a partisan, for he had never been a Republican, but only to do all he could in "helping to save the country." The manner in which Lincoln succeeded in taming this lion to his will, by frankly recognizing his great qualities, by giving him the most generous confidence, by aiding him in his work to the full of his power, by kindly concession or affectionate persuasiveness in cases of differing opinions, or, when it was necessary, by firm assertions of superior authority, bears the highest testimony to his skill in the management of men. Stanton, who had entered the service with rather a mean opinion of Lincoln's character and capacity, became one of his warmest, most devoted, and most admiring friends, and with none of his secretaries was Lincoln's intercourse more intimate. To take advice with candid readiness, and to weigh it without any pride of his own opinion, was one of Lincoln's preëminent virtues; but he had not long presided over his cabinet council when his was felt by all its members to be the ruling mind.

The cautious policy foreshadowed in his inaugural address, and pursued during the first period of the civil war, was far from satisfying all his party friends. The ardent spirits among the Union men thought that the whole North should at once be called to arms, to crush the rebellion by one powerful blow. The ardent spirits among the anti-slavery men insisted that, slavery having brought forth the rebellion, this powerful blow should at once be aimed at slavery. Both complained that the administration was spiritless, undecided, and lamentably slow in its proceedings. Lincoln reasoned otherwise. The ways of thinking and feeling of the masses, of the plain people, were constantly present to his mind. The masses, the plain people, had to furnish the men for the fighting, if fighting was to be done. He believed that the plain people would be ready to fight when it clearly appeared necessary, and that they would feel that necessity when they felt themselves attacked. He therefore waited until the enemies of the Union struck the first blow. As soon as, on the 12th of April, 1861, the first gun was fired in Charleston harbor on the Union flag upon Fort Sumter, the call was sounded, and the Northern people rushed to arms.

Lincoln knew that the plain people were now indeed ready to fight in defence of the Union, but not yet ready to fight for the destruction of slavery. He declared openly that he had a right to summon the people to fight for the Union, but not to summon them to fight for the abolition of slavery as a primary object; and this declaration gave him numberless soldiers for the Union who at that period would have hesitated to do battle against the institution of slavery. For a time he succeeded in rendering harmless the cry of the partisan opposition that the Republican administration was perverting the war for the Union into an "abolition war." But when he went so far as to countermand the acts of some generals in the field, looking to the emancipation of the slaves in the districts covered by their commands, loud complaints arose from earnest anti-slavery men, who accused the President of turning his back upon the anti-slavery cause. Many of these anti-slavery men will now, after a calm retrospect, be willing to admit that it would have been a hazardous policy to endanger, by precipitating a demonstrative fight against slavery, the success of the struggle for the Union.

Lincoln's views and feelings concerning slavery had not changed. Those who conversed with him intimately upon the subject at that period know that he did not expect slavery long to survive the triumph of the Union, even if it were not immediately destroyed by the war. In this he was right. Had the Union armies achieved a decisive victory in an early period of the conflict, and had the seceded States been received back with slavery, the "slave power" would then have been a defeated power,—defeated in an attempt to carry out its most effective threat. It would have lost its prestige. Its menaces would have been hollow sound, and ceased to make any one afraid. It could no longer have hoped to expand, to maintain an equilibrium in any branch of Congress, and to control the government. The victorious free States would have largely overbalanced it. It would no longer have been able to withstand the onset of a hostile age. It could no longer have ruled,—and slavery had to rule in order to live. It would have lingered for a while, but it would surely have been "in the course of ultimate extinction." A prolonged war precipitated the destruction of slavery; a short war might only have prolonged its death struggle. Lincoln saw this clearly; but he saw also that, in a protracted death struggle, it might still have kept disloyal sentiments alive, bred distracting commotions, and caused great mischief to the country. He therefore hoped that slavery would not survive the war.

But the question how he could rightfully employ his power to bring on its speedy destruction was to him not a question of mere sentiment. He himself set forth his reasoning upon it, at a later period, in one of his inimitable letters. "I am naturally anti-slavery," said he. "If slavery is not wrong, nothing is wrong. I cannot remember the time when I did not so think and feel. And yet I have never understood that the presidency conferred upon me an unrestricted right to act upon that judgment and feeling. It was in the oath I took that I would, to the best of my ability, preserve, protect, and defend the Constitution of the United States. I could not take the office without taking the oath. Nor was it my view that I might take an oath to get power, and break the oath in using that power. I understood, too, that, in ordinary civil administration, this oath even forbade me practically to indulge my private abstract judgment on the moral question of slavery. I did understand, however, also, that my oath imposed upon me the duty of preserving, to the best of my ability, by every indispensable means, that government, that nation, of which the Constitution was the organic law. I could not feel that, to the best of my ability, I had even *tried* to preserve the Constitution if, to save slavery, or any minor matter, I should permit the wreck of government, country, and Constitution all together." In other words, if the salvation of the government, the Constitution, and the Union demanded the destruction of slavery, he felt it to be not only his right, but his sworn duty to destroy it. Its destruction became a necessity of the war for the Union.

As the war dragged on and disaster followed disaster, the sense of that necessity steadily grew upon him. Early in 1862, as some of his friends well remember, he saw, what Seward seemed not to see, that to give the war for the Union an antislavery character was the surest means to prevent the recognition of the Southern Confederacy as an independent nation by European powers; that, slavery being abhorred by the moral sense of civilized mankind, no European government would dare to offer so gross an insult to the public opinion of its people as openly to favor the creation of a state founded upon slavery to the prejudice of an existing nation fighting against slavery. He saw also that slavery untouched was to the rebellion an element of power, and that in order to overcome that power it was necessary to turn it into an element of weakness. Still, he felt no assurance that the plain people were prepared for so radical a measure as the emancipation of the slaves by act of the government, and he anxiously considered that, if they were not, this great step might, by exciting dissension at the North, injure the cause of the Union in one quarter more than it would help it in another. He heartily welcomed an effort made in New York to mould and stimulate public sentiment on the slavery question by public meetings boldly pronouncing for emancipation. At the same time he himself cautiously advanced with a recommendation, expressed in a special message to Congress, that the United States should coöperate with any State which might adopt the gradual abolishment of slavery, giving such State pecuniary aid to compensate the former owners of emancipated slaves. The discussion was started, and spread rapidly. Congress adopted the resolution re-commended, and soon went a step farther in passing a bill to abolish slavery in the District of Columbia. The plain people began to look at emancipation on a larger scale, as a thing to be considered seriously by patriotic citizens; and soon Lincoln thought that the time was ripe, and that the edict of freedom could be ventured upon without danger of serious confusion in the Union ranks.

The failure of McClellan's movement upon Richmond increased immensely the prestige of the enemy. The need of some great act to stimulate the vitality of the Union cause seemed to grow daily more pressing. On July 21, 1862, Lincoln surprised his cabinet with the draught of a proclamation declaring free the slaves in all the States that should be still in rebellion against the United States on the 1st of January, 1863. As to the matter itself he announced that he had fully made up his mind; he invited advice only concerning the form and the time of publication. Seward suggested that the proclamation, if then brought out, amidst disaster and distress, would sound like the last shriek of a perishing cause. Lincoln accepted the suggestion, and the proclamation was postponed. Another defeat followed, the second at Bull Run. But when, after that battle, the Confederate army, under Lee, crossed the Potomac and invaded Maryland, Lincoln vowed in his heart that, if the Union army were now blessed with success, the decree of freedom should surely be issued. The victory of Antietam was won on September 17, and the preliminary Emancipation Proclamation came forth on the 22d. It was Lincoln's own resolution and act; but practically it bound the nation, and permitted no step backward. In spite of its limitations, it was the actual abolition of slavery. Thus he wrote his name upon the books of history with the title dearest to his heart,—the liberator of the slave.

It is true, the great proclamation, which stamped the war as one for "union and freedom," did not at once mark the turning of the tide on the field of military operations. There were more disasters,—Fredericksburg and Chancellorsville. But with Gettysburg and Vicksburg the whole aspect of the war changed. Step by step, now more slowly, then more rapidly, but with increasing steadiness, the flag of the

Union advanced from field to field toward the final consummation. The decree of emancipation was naturally followed by the enlistment of emancipated negroes in the Union armies. This measure had a farther reaching effect than merely giving the Union armies an increased supply of men. The laboring force of the rebellion was hopelessly disorganized. The war became like a problem of arithmetic. As the Union armies pushed forward, the area from which the Southern Confederacy could draw recruits and supplies constantly grew smaller, while the area from which the Union recruited its strength constantly grew larger: and everywhere, even within the Southern lines, the Union had its allies. The fate of the rebellion was then virtually decided; but it still required much bloody work to convince the brave warriors who fought for it that they were really beaten.

Neither did the Emancipation Proclamation[Footnote 1: The text of the Emancipation Proclamation will be found in Number 32, Riverside Literature series.] forthwith command universal assent among the people who were loyal to the Union. There were even signs of a reaction against the administration in the fall elections of 1862, seemingly justifying the opinion, entertained by many, that the President had really anticipated the development of popular feeling. The cry that the war for the Union had been turned into an "abolition war" was raised again by the opposition, and more loudly than ever. But the good sense and patriotic instincts of the plain people gradually marshalled themselves on Lincoln's side, and he lost no opportunity to help on this process by personal argument and admonition. There never has been a President in such constant and active contact with the public opinion of the country, as there never has been a President who, while at the head of the government, remained so near to the people. Beyond the circle of those who had long known him, the feeling steadily grew that the man in the White House was "honest Abe Lincoln" still, and that every citizen might approach him with complaint, expostulation, or advice, without danger of meeting a rebuff from power-proud authority or humiliating condescension; and this privilege was used by so many and with such unsparing freedom that only superhuman patience could have endured it all. There are men now living who would to-day read with amazement, if not regret, what they then ventured to say or write to him. But Lincoln repelled no one whom he believed to speak to him in good faith and with patriotic purpose. No good advice would go unheeded. No candid criticism would offend him. No honest opposition, while it might pain him, would produce a lasting alienation of feeling between him and the opponent. It may truly be said that few men in power have ever been exposed to more daring attempts to direct their course, to severer censure of their acts, and to more cruel misrepresentation of their motives. And all this he met with that good-natured humor peculiarly his own, and with untiring effort to see the right and to impress it upon those who differed from him. The conversations he had and the correspondence he carried on upon matters of public interest, not only with men in official position, but with private citizens, were almost unceasing, and in a large number of public letters, written ostensibly to meetings, or committees, or persons of importance, he addressed himself directly to the popular mind. Most of these letters stand among the finest monuments of our political literature. Thus he presented the singular spectacle of a President who, in the midst of a great civil war, with unprecedented duties weighing upon him, was constantly in person debating the great features of his policy with the people.

While in this manner he exercised an ever-increasing influence upon the popular understanding, his sympathetic nature endeared him more and more to the popular heart. In vain did journals and speakers of the opposition represent him as a light-minded trifler, who amused himself with frivolous story-telling and coarse jokes, while the blood of the people was flowing in streams. The people knew that the man at the head of affairs, on whose haggard face the twinkle of humor so frequently changed into an expression of profoundest sadness, was more than any other deeply distressed by the suffering he witnessed; that he felt the pain of every wound that was inflicted on the battlefield, and the anguish of every woman or child who had lost husband or father; that whenever he could he was eager to alleviate sorrow, and that his mercy was never implored in vain. They looked to him as one who was with them and of them in all their hopes and fears, their joys and sorrows,—who laughed with them and wept with them; and as his heart was theirs, so their hearts turned to him. His popularity was far different from that of Washington, who was revered with awe, or that of Jackson, the unconquerable hero, for whom party enthusiasm never grew weary of shouting. To Abraham Lincoln the people became bound by a genuine sentimental attachment. It was not a matter of respect, or confidence, or party pride, for this feeling spread far beyond the boundary lines of his party; it was an affair of the heart, independent of mere reasoning.

When the soldiers in the field or their folks at home spoke of "Father Abraham," there was no cant in it. They felt that their President was really caring for them as a father would, and that they could go to him, every one of them, as they would go to a father, and talk to him of what troubled them, sure to find a willing ear and tender sympathy. Thus, their President, and his cause, and his endeavors, and his success gradually became to them almost matters of family concern. And this popularity carried him triumphantly through the presidential election of 1864, in spite of an opposition within his own party which at first seemed very formidable.

Many of the radical anti-slavery men were never quite satisfied with Lincoln's ways of meeting the problems of the time. They were very earnest and mostly very able men, who had positive ideas as to "how this rebellion should be put down." They would not recognize the necessity of measuring the steps of the government according to the progress of opinion among the plain people. They criticised Lincoln's cautious management as irresolute, halting, lacking in definite purpose and in energy; he should not have delayed emancipation so long; he should not have confided important commands to men of doubtful views as to slavery; he should have authorized military commanders to set the slaves free as they went on; he dealt too leniently with unsuccessful generals; he should have put down all factious opposition with a strong hand instead of trying to pacify it; he should have given the people accomplished facts instead of arguing with them, and so on. It is true, these criticisms were not always entirely unfounded. Lincoln's policy had, with the virtues of democratic government, some of its weaknesses, which in the presence of pressing exigencies were apt to deprive governmental action of the necessary vigor; and his kindness of heart, his disposition always to respect the feelings of others, frequently made him recoil from anything like severity, even when severity was urgently called for. But many of his radical critics have since then revised their judgment sufficiently to admit that Lincoln's policy was, on the whole, the wisest and safest; that a policy of heroic methods, while it has sometimes accomplished great results, could in a democracy like ours be maintained only by constant success; that it would have quickly broken down under the weight of disaster; that it might have been successful from the start, had the Union, at the beginning of the conflict, had its Grants and Shermans and Sheridans, its Farraguts and Porters, fully matured at the head of its forces; but that, as the great commanders had to be evolved slowly from the developments of the war, constant success could not be counted upon, and it was best to follow a policy which was in friendly contact with the popular force, and therefore more fit to stand the trial of misfortune on the battlefield. But at that period they thought differently, and their dissatisfaction with Lincoln's doings was greatly increased by the steps he took toward the reconstruction of rebel States then partially in possession of the Union forces.

In December, 1863, Lincoln issued an amnesty proclamation, offering pardon to all implicated in the rebellion, with certain specified exceptions, on condition of their taking and maintaining an oath to support the Constitution and obey the laws of the United States and the proclamations of the President with regard to slaves; and also promising that when, in any of the rebel States, a number of citizens equal to one tenth of the voters in 1860 should reëstablish a state government in conformity with the oath above mentioned, such should be recognized by the Executive as the true government of the State. The proclamation seemed at first to be received with general favor. But soon another scheme of reconstruction, much more stringent in its provisions, was put forward in the House of Representatives by Henry Winter Davis. Benjamin Wade championed it in the Senate. It passed in the closing moments of the session in July, 1864, and Lincoln, instead of making it a law by his signature, embodied the text of it in a proclamation as a plan of reconstruction worthy of being earnestly considered. The differences of opinion concerning this subject had only intensified the feeling against Lincoln which had long been nursed among the radicals, and some of them openly declared their purpose of resisting his reëlection to the presidency. Similar sentiments were manifested by the advanced anti-slavery men of Missouri, who, in their hot faction-fight with the "conservatives" of that State, had not received from Lincoln the active support they demanded. Still another class of Union men, mainly in the East, gravely shook their heads when considering the question whether Lincoln should be reelected. They were those who cherished in their minds an ideal of statesmanship and of personal bearing in high office with which, in their opinion, Lincoln's individuality was much out of accord. They were shocked when they heard him cap an argument upon grave affairs of state with a story about "a man out in Sangamon County,"—a story, to be sure, strikingly clinching his point, but sadly lacking in dignity. They could not understand the man who was capable, in opening a cabinet meeting, of reading to his secretaries a funny chapter from a recent book of Artemus Ward, with which in an unoccupied moment he had relieved his care-burdened mind, and who then solemnly informed the executive council that he had vowed in his heart to issue a proclamation emancipating the slaves as soon as God blessed the Union arms with another victory. They were alarmed at the weakness of a President who would indeed resist the urgent remonstrances of statesmen against his policy, but could not resist the prayer of an old woman for the pardon of a soldier who was sentenced to be shot for desertion. Such men, mostly sincere and ardent patriots, not only wished, but earnestly set to work, to prevent Lincoln's renomination. Not a few of them actually believed, in 1863, that, if the national convention of the Union party were held then, Lincoln would not be supported by the delegation of a single State. But when the convention met at Baltimore, in June, 1864, the voice of the people was heard. On the first ballot Lincoln received the votes of the delegations from all the States except Missouri; and even the Missourians turned over their votes to him before the result of the ballot was declared.

But even after his renomination, the opposition to Lincoln within the ranks of the Union party did not subside. A convention, called by the dissatisfied radicals in Missouri, and favored by men of a similar way of thinking in other States, had been held already in May, and had nominated as its candidate for the presidency General Frémont. He, indeed, did not attract a strong following, but opposition movements from different quarters appeared more formidable. Henry Winter Davis and Benjamin Wade assailed Lincoln in a flaming manifesto. Other Union men, of undoubted patriotism and high standing, persuaded themselves, and sought to persuade the people, that Lincoln's renomination was ill advised and dangerous to the Union cause. As the Democrats had put off their convention until the 29th of August, the Union party had, during the larger part of the summer, no opposing candidate and platform to attack, and the political campaign languished. Neither were the tidings from the theatre of war of a cheering character. The terrible losses suffered by Grant's army in the battles of the Wilderness spread general gloom. Sherman seemed for a while to be in a precarious position before Atlanta. The opposition to Lincoln within the Union party grew louder in its complaints and discouraging predictions. Earnest demands were heard that his candidacy should be withdrawn. Lincoln himself, not knowing how strongly the masses were attached to him, was haunted by dark forebodings of defeat. Then the scene suddenly changed as if by magic. The Democrats, in their national convention, declared the war a failure, demanded, substantially, peace at any price, and nominated on such a platform General McClellan as their candidate. Their convention had hardly adjourned when the capture of Atlanta gave a new aspect to the military situation. It was like a sun-ray bursting through a dark cloud. The rank and file of the Union party rose with rapidly growing enthusiasm. The song "We are coming, Father Abraham, three hundred thousand strong," resounded all over the land. Long before the decisive day arrived, the result was beyond doubt, and Lincoln was reelected President by overwhelming majorities. The election over, even his severest critics found themselves forced to admit that Lincoln was the only possible candidate for the Union party in 1864, and that neither political combinations nor campaign speeches, nor even victories in the field, were needed to insure his success. The plain people had all the while been satisfied with Abraham Lincoln: they confided in him; they loved him; they felt themselves near to him; they saw personified in him the cause of Union and freedom; and they went to the ballot-box for him in their strength.

The hour of triumph called out the characteristic impulses of his nature. The opposition within the Union party had stung him to the quick. Now he had his opponents before him, baffled and humiliated. Not a moment did he lose to stretch out the hand of friendship to all. "Now that the election is over," he said, in response to a serenade, "may not all, having a common interest, reunite in a common effort to save our common country? For my own part, I have striven, and will strive, to place no obstacle in the way. So long as I have been here I have not willingly planted a thorn in any man's bosom. While I am deeply sensible to the high compliment of a reëlection, it adds nothing to my satisfaction that any other man may be pained or disappointed by the result. May I ask those who were with me to join with me in the same spirit toward those who were against me?" This was Abraham Lincoln's character as tested in the furnace of prosperity.

The war was virtually decided, but not yet ended. Sherman was irresistibly carrying the Union flag through the South. Grant had his iron hand upon the ramparts of Richmond. The days of the Confederacy were evidently numbered. Only the last blow remained to be struck. Then Lincoln's second inauguration came, and with it his second inaugural address. Lincoln's famous "Gettysburg speech"[Footnote 1:

Both the second inaugural address and the Gettysburg speech are printed in No. 32, Riverside Literature series.] has been much and justly admired. But far greater, as well as far more characteristic, was that inaugural in which he poured out the whole devotion and tenderness of his great soul. It had all the solemnity of a father's last admonition and blessing to his children before he lay down to die. These were its closing words: "Fondly do we hope, fervently do we pray, that this mighty scourge of war may speedily pass away. Yet if God wills that it continue until all the wealth piled up by the bondman's two hundred and fifty years of unrequited toil shall be sunk, and until every drop of blood drawn with the lash shall be paid by another drawn with the sword, as was said three thousand years ago, so still it must be said, 'The judgments of the Lord are true and righteous altogether.' With malice toward none, with charity for all, with firmness in the right as God gives us to see the right, let us strive to finish the work we are in; to bind up the nation's wounds; to care for him who shall have borne the battle, and for his widow and his orphan; to do all which may achieve and cherish a just and lasting peace among ourselves and with all nations."

This was like a sacred poem. No American President had ever spoken words like these to the American people. America never had a President who found such words in the depth of his heart.

Now followed the closing scenes of the war. The Southern armies fought bravely to the last, but all in vain. Richmond fell. Lincoln himself entered the city on foot, accompanied only by a few officers and a squad of sailors who had rowed him ashore from the flotilla in the James River, a negro picked up on the way serving as a guide. Never had the world seen a more modest conqueror and a more characteristic triumphal procession,—no army with banners and drums, only a throng of those who had been slaves, hastily run together, escorting the victorious chief into the capital of the vanquished foe. We are told that they pressed around him, kissed his hands and his garments, and shouted and danced for joy, while tears ran down the President's care-furrowed cheeks.

A few days more brought the surrender of Lee's army, and peace was assured. The people of the North were wild with joy. Everywhere festive guns were booming, bells pealing, the churches ringing with thanksgivings, and jubilant multitudes thronging the thoroughfares, when suddenly the news flashed over the land that

Abraham Lincoln had been murdered. The people were stunned by the blow. Then a wail of sorrow went up such as America had never heard before. Thousands of Northern households grieved as if they had lost their dearest member. Many a Southern man cried out in his heart that his people had been robbed of their best friend in their humiliation and distress, when Abraham Lincoln was struck down. It was as if the tender affection which his countrymen bore him had inspired all nations with a common sentiment. All civilized mankind stood mourning around the coffin of the dead President. Many of those, here and abroad, who not long before had ridiculed and reviled him were among the first to hasten on with their flowers of eulogy, and in that universal chorus of lamentation and praise there was not a voice that did not tremble with genuine emotion. Never since Washington's death had there been such unanimity of judgment as to a man's virtues and greatness; and even Washington's death, although his name was held in greater reverence, did not touch so sympathetic a chord in the people's hearts.

Nor can it be said that this was owing to the tragic character of Lincoln's end. It is true, the death of this gentlest and most merciful of rulers by the hand of a mad fanatic was well apt to exalt him beyond his merits in the estimation of those who loved him, and to make his renown the object of peculiarly tender solicitude. But it is also true that the verdict pronounced upon him in those days has been affected little by time, and that historical inquiry has served rather to increase than to lessen the appreciation of his virtues, his abilities, his services. Giving the fullest measure of credit to his great ministers,—to Seward for his conduct of foreign affairs, to Chase for the management of the finances under terrible difficulties, to Stanton for the performance of his tremendous task as war secretary,—and readily acknowledging that without the skill and fortitude of the great commanders, and the heroism of the soldiers and sailors under them, success could not have been achieved, the historian still finds that Lincoln's judgment and will were by no means governed by those around him; that the most important steps were owing to his initiative; that his was the deciding and directing mind; and that it was preeminently he whose sagacity and whose character enlisted for the administration in its struggles the countenance, the sympathy, and the support of the people. It is found, even, that his judgment on military matters was astonishingly acute, and that the advice and instructions he gave to the generals commanding in the field would not seldom have done honor to the ablest of them. History, therefore, without overlooking or palliating or excusing any of his shortcomings or mistakes, continues to place him foremost among the saviours of the Union and the liberators of the slave. More than that, it awards to him the merit of having accomplished what but few political philosophers would have recognized as possible,—of leading the republic through four years of furious civil conflict without any serious detriment to its free institutions.

He was, indeed, while President, violently denounced by the opposition as a tyrant and a usurper, for having gone beyond his constitutional powers in authorizing or permitting the temporary suppression of newspapers, and in wantonly suspending the writ of habeas corpus and resorting to arbitrary arrests Nobody should be blamed who, when such things are done, in good faith and from patriotic motives protests against them. In a republic, arbitrary stretches of power, even when demanded by necessity, should never be permitted to pass without a protest on the one hand, and without an apology on the other. It is well they did not so pass during our civil war. That arbitrary measures were resorted to, is true. That they were resorted to most sparingly, and only when the government thought them absolutely required by the safety of the republic, will now hardly be denied. But certain it is that the history of the world does not furnish a single example of a government passing through so tremendous a crisis as our civil war was with so small a record of arbitrary acts, and so little interference with the ordinary course of law outside the field of military operations. No American President ever wielded such power as that which was thrust into Lincoln's hands. It is to be hoped that no American President ever will have to be intrusted with such power again. But no man was ever intrusted with it to whom its seductions were less dangerous than they proved to be to Abraham Lincoln. With scrupulous care he endeavored, even under the most trying circumstances, to remain strictly within the constitutional limitations of his authority; and whenever the boundary became indistinct, or when the dangers of the situation forced him to cross it, he was equally careful to mark his acts as exceptional measures, justifiable only by the imperative necessities of the civil war, so that they might not pass into history as precedents for similar acts in time of peace. It is an unquestionable fact that during the reconstruction period which followed the war, more things were done capable of serving as dangerous precedents than during the war itself. Thus it may truly be said of him not only that under his guidance the republic was saved from disruption and the country was purified of the blot of slavery, but that, during the stormiest and most perilous crisis in our history, he so conducted the government and so wielded his almost dictatorial power as to leave essentially intact our free institutions in all things that concern the rights and liberties of the citizen .He understood well the nature of the problem. In his first message to Congress he defined it in admirably pointed language: "Must a government be of necessity too strong for the liberties of its own people, or too weak to maintain its own existence? Is there in all republics this inherent weakness?" This question he answered in the name of the great American republic, as no man could have answered it better, with a triumphant "No."

It has been said that Abraham Lincoln died at the right moment for his fame. However that may be, he had, at the time of his death, certainly not exhausted his usefulness to his country. He was probably the only man who could have guided the nation through the perplexities of the reconstruction period in such a manner as to prevent in the work of peace the revival of the passions of the war. He would indeed not have escaped serious controversy as to details of policy; but he could have weathered it far better than any other statesman of his time, for his prestige with the active politicians had been immensely strengthened by his triumphant reëlection; and what is more important, he would have been supported by the confidence of the victorious Northern people that he would do all to secure the safety of the Union and the rights of the emancipated negro, and at the same time by the confidence of the defeated Southern people that nothing would be done by him from motives of vindictiveness, or of unreasonable fanaticism, or of a selfish party spirit. "With malice toward none, with charity for all," the foremost of the victors would have personified in himself the genius of reconciliation.

He might have rendered the country a great service in another direction. A few days after the fall of Richmond, he pointed out to a friend the crowd of office-seekers besieging his door. "Look at that," said he. "Now we have conquered the rebellion, but here you see something that may become more dangerous to this republic than the rebellion itself." It is true, Lincoln as President did not profess what we now call civil service reform principles. He used the patronage of the government in many cases avowedly to reward party work, in many others to form combinations and to produce political effects advantageous to the Union cause, and in still others simply to put the right man into the right place. But in his endeavors to strengthen the Union cause, and in his search for able and useful men for public duties, he frequently went beyond the limits of his party, and gradually accustomed himself to the thought that, while party service had its value, considerations of the public interest were, as to appointments to office, of far greater consequence. Moreover, there had been such a mingling of different political elements in support of the Union during the civil war that Lincoln, standing at the head of that temporarily united motley mass, hardly felt himself, in the narrow sense of the term, a party man. And as he became strongly impressed with the dangers brought upon the republic by the use of public offices as party spoils, it is by no means improbable that had he survived the all-absorbing crisis and found time to turn to other objects, one of the most important reforms of later days would have been pioneered by his powerful authority. This was not to be. But the measure of his achievements was full enough for immortality.

To the younger generation Abraham Lincoln has already become a half-mythical figure, which, in the haze of historic distance, grows to more and more heroic proportions, but also loses in distinctness of outline and feature. This is indeed the common lot of popular heroes; but the Lincoln legend will be more than ordinarily apt to become fanciful, as his individuality, assembling seemingly incongruous qualities and forces in a character at the same time grand and most lovable, was so unique, and his career so abounding in startling contrasts. As the state of society in which Abraham Lincoln grew up passes away, the world will read with increasing wonder of the man who, not only of the humblest origin, but remaining the simplest and most unpretending of citizens, was raised to a position of power unprecedented in our history; who was the gentlest and most peace-loving of mortals, unable to see any creature suffer without a pang in his own breast, and suddenly found himself called to conduct the greatest and bloodiest of our wars; who wielded the power of government when stern resolution and relentless force were the order of the day, and then won and ruled the popular mind and heart by the tender sympathies of his nature; who was a cautious conservative by temperament and mental habit, and led the most sudden and sweeping social revolution of our time; who, preserving his homely speech and rustic manner even in the most conspicuous position of that period, drew upon himself the scoffs of polite society, and then thrilled the soul of mankind with utterances of wonderful beauty and grandeur; who, in his heart the best friend of the defeated South, was murdered because a crazy fanatic took him for its most cruel enemy; who, while in power, was beyond measure lampooned and maligned by sectional passion and an excited party spirit, and around whose bier friend and foe gathered to praise him—which they have since never ceased to do—as one of the greatest of Americans and the best of men.

REMARKS AT THE FUNERAL SERVICES HELD IN CONCORD, APRIL 19, 1865.

BY RALPH WALDO EMERSON.

WE meet under the gloom of a calamity which darkens down over the minds of good men in all civil society, as the fearful tidings travel over sea, over land, from country to country, like the shadow of an uncalculated eclipse over the planet. Old as history is, and manifold as are its tragedies, I doubt if any death has caused so much pain to mankind as this has caused, or will cause, on its announcement; and this, not so much because nations are by modern arts brought so closely together, as because of the mysterious hopes and fears which, in the present day, are connected with the name and institutions of America.

In this country, on Saturday, every one was struck dumb, and saw at first only deep below deep, as he meditated on the ghastly blow. And perhaps, at this hour, when the coffin which contains the dust of the President sets forward on its long march through mourning States, on its way to his home in Illinois, we might well be silent, and suffer the awful voices of the time to thunder to us. Yes, but that first despair was brief: the man was not so to be mourned. He was the most active and hopeful of men; and his work had not perished: but acclamations of praise for the task he had accomplished burst out into a song of triumph, which even tears for his death cannot keep down.

The President stood before us as a man of the people. He was thoroughly American, had never crossed the sea, had never been spoiled by English insularity or French dissipation; a quite native, aboriginal man, as an acorn from the oak; no aping of foreigners, no frivolous accomplishments, Kentuckian born, working on a farm, a flatboat-man, a captain in the Black Hawk war, a country lawyer, a representative in the rural legislature of Illinois;—on such modest foundations the broad structure of his fame was laid. How slowly, and yet by happily prepared steps, he came to his place. All of us remember—it is only a history of five or six years—the surprise and the disappointment of the country at his first nomination by the convention at Chicago. Mr. Seward, then in the culmination of his good fame, was the favorite of the Eastern States. And when the new and comparatively unknown name of Lincoln was announced (notwithstanding the report of the acclamations of that convention), we heard the result coldly and sadly. It seemed too rash, on a purely local reputation, to build so grave a trust in such anxious times; and men naturally talked of the chances in politics as incalculable. But it turned out not to be chance. The profound good opinion which the people of Illinois and of the West had conceived of him, and which they had imparted to their colleagues, that they also might justify themselves to their constituents at home, was not rash, though they did not begin to know the riches of his worth.

A plain man of the people, an extraordinary fortune attended him. He offered no shining qualities at the first encounter; he did not offend by superiority. He had a face and manner which disarmed suspicion, which inspired confidence, which confirmed good will. He was a man without vices. He had a strong sense of duty, which it was very easy for him to obey. Then he had what farmers call a long head; was excellent in working out the sum for himself; in arguing his case and convincing you fairly and firmly. Then it turned out that he was a great worker; had prodigious faculty of performance; worked easily. A good worker is so rare; everybody has some disabling quality. In a host of young men that start together and promise so many brilliant leaders for the next age, each fails on trial; one by bad health, one by conceit, or by love of pleasure, or lethargy, or an ugly temper,—each has some disqualifying fault that throws him out of the career. But this man was sound to the core, cheerful, persistent, all right for labor, and liked nothing so well.

Then he had a vast good nature, which made him tolerant and accessible to all; fair minded, leaning to the claim of the petitioner; affable, and not sensible to the affliction which the innumerable visits paid to him when President would have brought to any one else. And how this good nature became a noble humanity, in many a tragic case which the events of the war brought to him, every one will remember; and with what increasing tenderness he dealt when a whole race was thrown on his compassion. The poor negro said of him, on an impressive occasion, "Massa Linkum am eberywhere."

Then his broad good humor, running easily into jocular talk, in which he delighted and in which he excelled, was a rich gift to this wise man. It enabled him to keep his secret; to meet every kind of man and every rank in society; to take off the edge of the severest decisions; to mask his own purpose and sound his companion; and to catch with true instinct the temper of every company he addressed. And, more than all, it is to a man of severe labor, in anxious and exhausting crises, the natural restorative, good as sleep, and is the protection of the overdriven brain against rancor and insanity.

He is the author of a multitude of good sayings, so disguised as pleasantries that it is certain they had no reputation at first but as jests; and only later, by the very acceptance and adoption they find in the mouths of millions, turn out to be the wisdom of the hour. I am sure if this man had ruled in a period of less facility of printing, he would have become mythological in a very few years, like Æsop or Pilpay, or one of the Seven Wise Masters, by his fables and proverbs. But the weight and penetration of many passages in his letters, messages, and speeches, hidden now by the very closeness of their application to the moment, are destined hereafter to wide fame. What pregnant definitions; what unerring common sense; what foresight; and, on great occasion, what lofty, and more than national, what humane tone! His brief speech at Gettysburg will not easily be surpassed by words on any recorded occasion. This, and one other American speech, that of John Brown to the court that tried him, and a part of Kossuth's speech at Birmingham, can only be compared with each other, and with no fourth.

His occupying the chair of State was a triumph of the good sense of mankind, and of the public conscience. This middle-class country had got a middle-class President, at last. Yes, in manners and sympathies, but not in powers, for his powers were superior. This man grew according to the need. His mind mastered the problem of the day; and as the problem grew, so did his comprehension of it. Rarely was man so fitted to the event. In the midst of fears and jealousies, in the Babel of counsels and parties, this man wrought incessantly with all his might and all his honesty, laboring to find what the people wanted, and how to obtain that. It cannot be said there is any exaggeration of his worth. If ever a man was fairly tested, he was. There was no lack of resistance, nor of slander, nor of ridicule. The times have allowed no state secrets; the nation has been in such ferment, such multitudes had to be trusted, that no secret could be kept. Every door was ajar, and we know all that befell.

Then, what an occasion was the whirlwind of the war. Here was place for no holiday magistrate, no fair-weather sailor; the new pilot was hurried to the helm in a tornado. In four years,—four years of battle-days,—his endurance, his fertility of resources, his magnanimity, were sorely tried and never found wanting. There, by his courage, his justice, his even temper, his fertile counsel, his humanity, he stood a heroic figure in the centre of a heroic epoch. He is the true history of the American people in his time. Step by step he walked before them; slow with their slowness, quickening his march by theirs, the true representative of this continent; an entirely public man; father of his country, the pulse of twenty millions throbbing in his heart, the thought of their minds articulated by his tongue.

Adam Smith remarks that the axe, which in Hou-braken's portraits of British kings and worthies is engraved under those who have suffered at the block, adds a certain lofty charm to the picture. And who does not see, even in this tragedy so recent, how fast the terror and ruin of the massacre are already burning into glory around the victim? Far happier this fate than to have lived to be wished away; to have watched the decay of his own faculties; to have seen—perhaps even he—the proverbial ingratitude of statesmen; to have seen mean men preferred. Had he not lived long enough to keep the greatest promise that ever man made to his fellow men,—the practical abolition of slavery? He had seen Tennessee, Missouri, and Maryland emancipate their slaves. He had seen Savannah, Charleston, and Richmond surrendered; had seen the main army of the rebellion lay down its arms. He had conquered the public opinion of Canada, England, and France. Only Washington can compare with him in fortune.

And what if it should turn out, in the unfolding of the web, that he had reached the term; that this heroic deliverer could no longer serve us; that the rebellion had touched its natural conclusion, and what remained to be done required new and uncommitted hands,—a new spirit born out of the ashes of the war; and that Heaven, wishing to show the world a completed benefactor, shall make him serve his country even more by his death than by his life? Nations, like kings, are not good by facility and complaisance. "The kindness of kings consists in justice and strength." Easy good nature has been the dangerous foible of the Republic, and it was necessary that its enemies should outrage it, and drive us to unwonted firmness, to secure the salvation of this country in the next ages.

The ancients believed in a serene and beautiful Genius which ruled in the affairs of nations; which, with a slow but stern justice, carried forward the fortunes of certain chosen houses, weeding out single offenders or offending families, and securing at last the firm prosperity of the favorites of Heaven. It was too narrow a view of the Eternal Nemesis. There is a serene Providence which rules the fate of nations, which makes little account of time, little of one generation or race, makes no account of disasters, conquers alike by what is called defeat or by what is called victory, thrusts aside enemy and obstruction, crushes everything immoral as inhuman, and obtains the ultimate triumph of the best race by the sacrifice of everything which resists the moral laws of the world. It makes its own instruments, creates the man for the time, trains him in poverty, inspires his genius, and arms him for his task. It has given every race its own talent, and ordains that only that race which combines perfectly with the virtues of all shall endure.

THE EMANCIPATION GROUP.
BY JOHN GEEENLEAF WHITTIER.

MOSES KIMBALL, a citizen of Boston, presented to the city a duplicate of the Freedman's Memorial Statue erected in Lincoln Square, Washington, after a design by Thomas Ball. The group, which stands in Park Square, represents the figure of a slave, from whose limbs the broken fetters have fallen, kneeling in gratitude at the feet of Lincoln. The verses which follow were written for the unveiling of the statue, December 9, 1879.

Amidst thy sacred effigies Of old renown give place, O city, Freedom-loved ! to his Whose hand unchained a race.

Take the worn frame, that rested not Save in a martyr's grave; The care-lined face, that none forgot, Bent to the kneeling slave.

Let man be free ! The mighty word He spake was not his own; An impulse from the Highest stirred These chiselled lips alone.

The cloudy sign, the fiery guide, Along his pathway ran, And Nature, Through his voice, denied The ownership of man.

We rest in peace where these sad eyes Saw peril, strife, and pain; His was the nation's sacrifice, And ours the priceless gain.

O Symbol of God's will on earth As it is done above! Bear witness to the cost and worth Of justice and of love.

Stand in thy place and testify To coming ages long, That truth is stronger than a lie, And righteousness than wrong.

FOR THE SEEVICES IN MEMOEY OF ABEAHAM LINCOLN.
CITY OF BOSTON, JUNE 1, 1865.
BY OLIVER WENDELL HOLMES.

CHORAL: "Luther's Judgment Hymn."
O THOU of soul and sense and breath The ever-present Giver, Unto thy mighty Angel, Death, All flesh thou dost deliver; What most we cherish we resign, For life and death alike are thine, Who reignest Lord forever!

Our hearts lie buried in the dust With him so true and tender, The patriot's stay, the people's trust, The shield of the offender; Yet every murmuring voice is still, As, bowing to thy sovereign will, Our best-loved we surrender.

Dear Lord, with pitying eye behold This martyr generation, Which thou, through trials manifold, Art showing thy salvation! Oh, let the blood by murder spilt Wash out thy stricken children's guilt, And sanctify our nation!

IN MEMORY OF LINCOLN.

Be thou thy orphaned Israel's friend, Forsake thy people never, In One our broken Many blend That none again may sever! Hear us, O Father, while we raise With trembling lips our song of praise, And bless thy name forever!

EXTRACT FROM ODE

RECITED AT THE HARVARD COMMEMORATION, JULY 21, 1865.

BY JAMES RUSSELL LOWELL.

V.

WHITHER leads the path To ampler fates that leads? Not down through flowery meads, To reap an aftermath Of youth's vainglorious weeds; But up the steep, amid the wrath And shock of deadly-hostile creeds, Where the world's best hope and stay By battle's flashes gropes a desperate way, And every turf the fierce foot clings to bleeds. Peace hath her not ignoble wreath, Ere yet the sharp, decisive word Light the black lips of cannon, and the sword Dreams in its easeful sheath; But some day the live coal behind the thought, Whether from Baal's stone obscene, Or from the shrine serene Of God's pure altar brought, Bursts up in flame; the war of tongue and pen Learns with what deadly purpose it was fraught, And, helpless in the fiery passion caught, Shakes all the pillared state with shock of men: Some day the soft Ideal that we wooed Confronts us fiercely, foe-beset, pursued, And cries reproachful: "Was it, then, my praise, And not myself was loved? Prove now thy truth; I claim of thee the promise of thy youth; Give me thy life, or cower in empty phrase, The victim of thy genius, not its mate!" Life may be given in many ways, And loyalty to Truth be sealed As bravely in the closet as the field, So bountiful is Fate; But then to stand beside her, When craven churls deride her, To front a lie in arms and not to yield, This shows, methinks, God's plan And measure of a stalwart man, Limbed like the old heroic breeds, Who stands self-poised on manhood's solid earth, Not forced to frame excuses for his birth, Fed from within with all the strength he needs.

VI.

Such was he, our Martyr-Chief, Whom late the Nation he had led, With ashes on her head, Wept with the passion of an angry grief: Forgive me, if from present things I turn To speak what in my heart will beat and burn, And hang my wreath on his world-honored urn. Nature, they say, doth dote, And cannot make a man Save on some worn-out plan, Repeating us by rote: For him her Old-World moulds aside she threw, And, choosing sweet clay from the breast Of the unexhausted West, With stuff untainted shaped a hero new, Wise, steadfast in the strength of God, and true. How beautiful to see Once more a shepherd of mankind indeed, Who loved his charge, but never loved to lead; One whose meek flock the people joyed to be, Not lured by any cheat of birth, But by his clear-grained human worth, And brave old wisdom of sincerity! They knew that outward grace is dust; They could not choose but trust In that sure-footed mind's unfaltering skill, And supple-tempered will That bent like perfect steel to spring again and thrust. His was no lonely mountain-peak of mind, Thrusting to thin air o'er our cloudy bars, A sea-mark now, now lost in vapors blind; Broad prairie rather, genial, level-lined, Fruitful and friendly for all human-kind, Yet also nigh to heaven and loved of loftiest stars. Nothing of Europe here, Or, then, of Europe fronting morn ward still, Ere any names of Serf and Peer Could Nature's equal scheme deface And thwart her genial will; Here was a type of the true elder race, And one of Plutarch's men talked with us face to face. I praise him not; it were too late; And some innative weakness there must be In him who condescends to victory Such as the Present gives, and cannot wait, Safe in himself as in a fate. So always firmly he: He knew to bide his time, And can his fame abide, Still patient in his simple faith sublime, Till the wise years decide. Great captains, with their guns and drums, Disturb our judgment for the hour, But at last silence comes; These all are gone, and, standing like a tower, Our children shall behold his fame, The kindly-earnest, brave, fore-seeing man, Sagacious, patient, dreading praise, not blame, New birth of our new soil, the first American.

The Codes Of Hammurabi And Moses
W. W. Davies

The discovery of the Hammurabi Code is one of the greatest achievements of archaeology, and is of paramount interest, not only to the student of the Bible, but also to all those interested in ancient history...

Religion **ISBN:** *1-59462-338-4* Pages:132 *MSRP $12.95*

The Theory of Moral Sentiments
Adam Smith

This work from 1749. contains original theories of conscience amd moral judgment and it is the foundation for systemof morals.

Philosophy **ISBN:** *1-59462-777-0* Pages:536 *MSRP $19.95*

Jessica's First Prayer
Hesba Stretton

In a screened and secluded corner of one of the many railway-bridges which span the streets of London there could be seen a few years ago, from five o'clock every morning until half past eight, a tidily set-out coffee-stall, consisting of a trestle and board, upon which stood two large tin cans, with a small fire of charcoal burning under each so as to keep the coffee boiling during the early hours of the morning when the work-people were thronging into the city on their way to their daily toil...

Childrens **ISBN:** *1-59462-373-2* Pages:84 *MSRP $9.95*

My Life and Work
Henry Ford

Henry Ford revolutionized the world with his implementation of mass production for the Model T automobile. Gain valuable business insight into his life and work with his own auto-biography... "We have only started on our development of our country we have not as yet, with all our talk of wonderful progress, done more than scratch the surface. The progress has been wonderful enough but..."

Biographies/ **ISBN:** *1-59462-198-5* Pages:300 *MSRP $21.95*

www.bookjungle.com email: sales@bookjungle.com fax: 630-214-0564 mail: Book Jungle PO Box 2226 Champaign, IL 61825

The Art of Cross-Examination
Francis Wellman

QTY

I presume it is the experience of every author, after his first book is published upon an important subject, to be almost overwhelmed with a wealth of ideas and illustrations which could readily have been included in his book, and which to his own mind, at least, seem to make a second edition inevitable. Such certainly was the case with me; and when the first edition had reached its sixth impression in five months, I rejoiced to learn that it seemed to my publishers that the book had met with a sufficiently favorable reception to justify a second and considerably enlarged edition. ..

Reference   ISBN: *1-59462-647-2*   Pages:412   MSRP $19.95

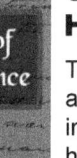

On the Duty of Civil Disobedience
Henry David Thoreau

QTY

Thoreau wrote his famous essay, On the Duty of Civil Disobedience, as a protest against an unjust but popular war and the immoral but popular institution of slave-owning. He did more than write—he declined to pay his taxes, and was hauled off to gaol in consequence. Who can say how much this refusal of his hastened the end of the war and of slavery ?

Law   ISBN: *1-59462-747-9*   Pages:48   MSRP $7.45

Dream Psychology Psychoanalysis for Beginners
Sigmund Freud

QTY

Sigmund Freud, born Sigismund Schlomo Freud (May 6, 1856 - September 23, 1939), was a Jewish-Austrian neurologist and psychiatrist who co-founded the psychoanalytic school of psychology. Freud is best known for his theories of the unconscious mind, especially involving the mechanism of repression; his redefinition of sexual desire as mobile and directed towards a wide variety of objects; and his therapeutic techniques, especially his understanding of transference in the therapeutic relationship and the presumed value of dreams as sources of insight into unconscious desires.

Psychology   ISBN: *1-59462-905-6*   Pages:196   MSRP $15.45

The Miracle of Right Thought
Orison Swett Marden

QTY

Believe with all of your heart that you will do what you were made to do. When the mind has once formed the habit of holding cheerful, happy, prosperous pictures, it will not be easy to form the opposite habit. It does not matter how improbable or how far away this realization may see, or how dark the prospects may be, if we visualize them as best we can, as vividly as possible, hold tenaciously to them and vigorously struggle to attain them, they will gradually become actualized, realized in the life. But a desire, a longing without endeavor, a yearning abandoned or held indifferently will vanish without realization.

Self Help   ISBN: *1-59462-644-8*   Pages:360   MSRP $25.45

www.bookjungle.com email: sales@bookjungle.com fax: 630-214-0564 mail: Book Jungle PO Box 2226 Champaign, IL 61825

QTY

☐	**The Rosicrucian Cosmo-Conception Mystic Christianity** *by Max Heindel* The Rosicrucian Cosmo-conception is not dogmatic, neither does it appeal to any other authority than the reason of the student. It is: not controversial, but is: sent forth in the, hope that it may help to clear... *New Age/Religion Pages 646*	ISBN: *1-59462-188-8*	$38.95
☐	**Abandonment To Divine Providence** *by Jean-Pierre de Caussade* "The Rev. Jean Pierre de Caussade was one of the most remarkable spiritual writers of the Society of Jesus in France in the 18th Century. His death took place at Toulouse in 1751. His works have gone through many editions and have been republished..." *Inspirational/Religion Pages 400*	ISBN: *1-59462-228-0*	$25.95
☐	**Mental Chemistry** *by Charles Haanel* Mental Chemistry allows the change of material conditions by combining and appropriately utilizing the power of the mind. Much like applied chemistry creates something new and unique out of careful combinations of chemicals the mastery of mental chemistry... *New Age Pages 354*	ISBN: *1-59462-192-6*	$23.95
☐	**The Letters of Robert Browning and Elizabeth Barret Barrett 1845-1846 vol II** *by Robert Browning and Elizabeth Barrett* *Biographies Pages 596*	ISBN: *1-59462-193-4*	$35.95
☐	**Gleanings In Genesis (volume I)** *by Arthur W. Pink* Appropriately has Genesis been termed "the seed plot of the Bible" for in it we have, in germ form, almost all of the great doctrines which are afterwards fully developed in the books of Scripture which follow... *Religion/Inspirational Pages 420*	ISBN: *1-59462-130-6*	$27.45
☐	**The Master Key** *by L. W. de Laurence* In no branch of human knowledge has there been a more lively increase of the spirit of research during the past few years than in the study of Psychology, Concentration and Mental Discipline. The requests for authentic lessons in Thought Control, Mental Discipline and... *New Age/Business Pages 422*	ISBN: *1-59462-001-6*	$30.95
☐	**The Lesser Key Of Solomon Goetia** *by L. W. de Laurence* This translation of the first book of the "Lemegton" which is now for the first time made accessible to students of Talismanic Magic was done, after careful collation and edition, from numerous Ancient Manuscripts in Hebrew, Latin, and French... *New Age/Occult Pages 92*	ISBN: *1-59462-092-X*	$9.95
☐	**Rubaiyat Of Omar Khayyam** *by Edward Fitzgerald* Edward Fitzgerald, whom the world has already learned, in spite of his own efforts to remain within the shadow of anonymity, to look upon as one of the rarest poets of the century, was born at Bredfield, in Suffolk, on the 31st of March, 1809. He was the third son of John Purcell... *Music Pages 172*	ISBN: *1-59462-332-5*	$13.95
☐	**Ancient Law** *by Henry Maine* The chief object of the following pages is to indicate some of the earliest ideas of mankind, as they are reflected in Ancient Law, and to point out the relation of those ideas to modern thought. *Religiom/History Pages 452*	ISBN: *1-59462-128-4*	$29.95
☐	**Far-Away Stories** *by William J. Locke* "Good wine needs no bush, but a collection of mixed vintages does. And this book is just such a collection. Some of the stories I do not want to remain buried for ever in the museum files of dead magazine-numbers an author's not unpardonable vanity..." *Fiction Pages 272*	ISBN: *1-59462-129-2*	$19.45
☐	**Life of David Crockett** *by David Crockett* "Colonel David Crockett was one of the most remarkable men of the times in which he lived. Born in humble life, but gifted with a strong will, an indomitable courage, and unremitting perseverance... *Biographies/New Age Pages 424*	ISBN: *1-59462-250-7*	$27.45
☐	**Lip-Reading** *by Edward Nitchie* Edward B. Nitchie, founder of the New York School for the Hard of Hearing, now the Nitchie School of Lip-Reading, Inc, wrote "LIP-READING Principles and Practice". The development and perfecting of this meritorious work on lip-reading was an undertaking... *How-to Pages 400*	ISBN: *1-59462-206-X*	$25.95
☐	**A Handbook of Suggestive Therapeutics, Applied Hypnotism, Psychic Science** *by Henry Munro* *Health/New Age/Health/Self-help Pages 376*	ISBN: *1-59462-214-0*	$24.95
☐	**A Doll's House: and Two Other Plays** *by Henrik Ibsen* Henrik Ibsen created this classic when in revolutionary 1848 Rome. Introducing some striking concepts in playwriting for the realist genre, this play has been studied the world over. *Fiction/Classics/Plays 308*	ISBN: *1-59462-112-8*	$19.95
☐	**The Light of Asia** *by sir Edwin Arnold* In this poetic masterpiece, Edwin Arnold describes the life and teachings of Buddha. The man who was to become known as Buddha to the world was born as Prince Gautama of India but he rejected the worldly riches and abandoned the reigns of power when... *Religion/History/Biographies Pages 170*	ISBN: *1-59462-204-3*	$13.95
☐	**The Complete Works of Guy de Maupassant** *by Guy de Maupassant* "For days and days, nights and nights, I had dreamed of that first kiss which was to consecrate our engagement, and I knew not on what spot I should put my lips..." *Fiction/Classics Pages 240*	ISBN: *1-59462-157-8*	$16.95
☐	**The Art of Cross-Examination** *by Francis L. Wellman* Written by a renowned trial lawyer, Wellman imparts his experience and uses case studies to explain how to use psychology to extract desired information through questioning. *How-to/Science/Reference Pages 408*	ISBN: *1-59462-309-0*	$26.95
☐	**Answered or Unanswered?** *by Louisa Vaughan* Miracles of Faith in China *Religion Pages 112*	ISBN: *1-59462-248-5*	$10.95
☐	**The Edinburgh Lectures on Mental Science (1909)** *by Thomas* This book contains the substance of a course of lectures recently given by the writer in the Queen Street Hall, Edinburgh. Its purpose is to indicate the Natural Principles governing the relation between Mental Action and Material Conditions... *New Age/Psychology Pages 148*	ISBN: *1-59462-008-3*	$11.95
☐	**Ayesha** *by H. Rider Haggard* Verily and indeed it is the unexpected that happens! Probably if there was one person upon the earth from whom the Editor of this, and of a certain previous history, did not expect to hear again... *Classics Pages 380*	ISBN: *1-59462-301-5*	$24.95
☐	**Ayala's Angel** *by Anthony Trollope* The two girls were both pretty, but Lucy who was twenty-one who supposed to be simple and comparatively unattractive, whereas Ayala was credited, as her Bombwhat romantic name might show, with poetic charm and a taste for romance. Ayala when her father died was nineteen... *Fiction Pages 484*	ISBN: *1-59462-352-X*	$29.95
☐	**The American Commonwealth** *by James Bryce* An interpretation of American democratic political theory. It examines political mechanics and society from the perspective of Scotsman James Bryce *Politics Pages 572*	ISBN: *1-59462-286-8*	$34.45
☐	**Stories of the Pilgrims** *by Margaret P. Pumphrey* This book explores pilgrims religious oppression in England as well as their escape to Holland and eventual crossing to America on the Mayflower, and their early days in New England... *History Pages 268*	ISBN: *1-59462-116-0*	$17.95

www.bookjungle.com email: sales@bookjungle.com fax: 630-214-0564 mail: Book Jungle PO Box 2226 Champaign, IL 61825

			QTY
The Fasting Cure by *Sinclair Upton*	ISBN: *1-59462-222-1*	**$13.95**	

In the Cosmopolitan Magazine for May, 1910, and in the Contemporary Review (London) for April, 1910, I published an article dealing with my experiences in fasting. I have written a great many magazine articles, but never one which attracted so much attention... *New Age/Self Help/Health Pages 164*

Hebrew Astrology by *Sepharial* — ISBN: *1-59462-308-2* **$13.45**

In these days of advanced thinking it is a matter of common observation that we have left many of the old landmarks behind and that we are now pressing forward to greater heights and to a wider horizon than that which represented the mind-content of our progenitors... *Astrology Pages 144*

Thought Vibration or The Law of Attraction in the Thought World — ISBN: *1-59462-127-6* **$12.95**
by *William Walker Atkinson* — *Psychology/Religion Pages 144*

Optimism by *Helen Keller* — ISBN: *1-59462-108-X* **$15.95**

Helen Keller was blind, deaf, and mute since 19 months old, yet famously learned how to overcome these handicaps, communicate with the world, and spread her lectures promoting optimism. An inspiring read for everyone... *Biographies/Inspirational Pages 84*

Sara Crewe by *Frances Burnett* — ISBN: *1-59462-360-0* **$9.45**

In the first place, Miss Minchin lived in London. Her home was a large, dull, tall one, in a large, dull square, where all the houses were alike, and all the sparrows were alike, and where all the door-knockers made the same heavy sound... *Childrens/Classic Pages 88*

The Autobiography of Benjamin Franklin by *Benjamin Franklin* — ISBN: *1-59462-135-7* **$24.95**

The Autobiography of Benjamin Franklin has probably been more extensively read than any other American historical work, and no other book of its kind has had such ups and downs of fortune. Franklin lived for many years in England, where he was agent... *Biographies/History Pages 332*

Name	
Email	
Telephone	
Address	
City, State ZIP	

☐ Credit Card   ☐ Check / Money Order

Credit Card Number	
Expiration Date	
Signature	

Please Mail to: Book Jungle
                    PO Box 2226
                    Champaign, IL 61825
or Fax to: 630-214-0564

ORDERING INFORMATION

web: *www.bookjungle.com*
email: *sales@bookjungle.com*
fax: *630-214-0564*
mail: *Book Jungle PO Box 2226 Champaign, IL 61825*
or PayPal *to sales@bookjungle.com*

Please contact us for bulk discounts

DIRECT-ORDER TERMS

**20% Discount if You Order
Two or More Books**
Free Domestic Shipping!
Accepted: Master Card, Visa,
Discover, American Express

www.ingramcontent.com/pod-product-compliance
Lightning Source LLC
Chambersburg PA
CBHW081328040426
42453CB00013B/2337